Into the Blue

FAMILY SECRETS AND THE SEARCH
FOR A GREAT LAKES
SHIPWRECK

Into the Blue

Andrea Curtis

RANDOM HOUSE CANADA

www.randomhouse.ca

National Library of Canada Cataloguing in Publication

Curtis, Andrea

Into the blue : family secrets and the search for a Great Lakes shipwreck /
Andrea Curtis.

ISBN 0–679–31135–1
1. J. H. Jones (Steamer) 2. Crawford family. 3. Shipwrecks—Ontario—
Georgian Bay (Bay)—History—19th century. 4. Georgian Bay Region
(Ont.)—History. 5. Shipwrecks—Great Lakes—History—19th century.
6. Wiarton (Ont.)—History. 7. Wiarton (Ont.)—Biography.
8. Curtis, Andrea—Family. I. Title.
FC3099.W523Z49 2003   971.3'1503   C2002–904544–4
F1059.5.W475C87 2002

Text design by CS Richardson

Printed in the United States of America

10 9 8 7 6 5 4 3 2 1

For my family

"Now I no longer believe that people's secrets are defined and communicable, or their feelings full-blown and easy to recognize. I don't believe so. Now, I can only say, my father's sisters . . . scrubbed the floor with lye . . ."

—"The Stone in the Field," Alice Munro

"The whole coast of this projecting Point being a steep rock Cliff without any Camp Ground or Landing Place is extremely dangerous for Boats or Canoes to go round and is therefore rarely attempted. Of those who have ventured several have perished."

—from a map of the Bruce Peninsula by Gother Mann, 1788

TABLE OF CONTENTS

PART I

Chapter 1	A Pirate on the Family Tree	3
Chapter 2	The Indian Peninsula	19
Chapter 3	Sawdust Town	33
Chapter 4	The Turkey Trail	49
Chapter 5	The Shipping News	59
Chapter 6	The Wildcat Whistle	75
Chapter 7	The Big Blow	93
Chapter 8	Red Sky in the Morning	113

PART II

Chapter 9	All Hands Lost	131
Chapter 10	The Saddest Calamity	151
Chapter 11	The Summer People	167
Chapter 12	The Locket	177
Chapter 13	In a Strange Land	205
Chapter 14	As Man and Wife	217
Chapter 15	The Gall	239
Chapter 16	"The deep waters of Georgian Bay never give up their dead"	257
	Image Credits	265
	Acknowledgements	267

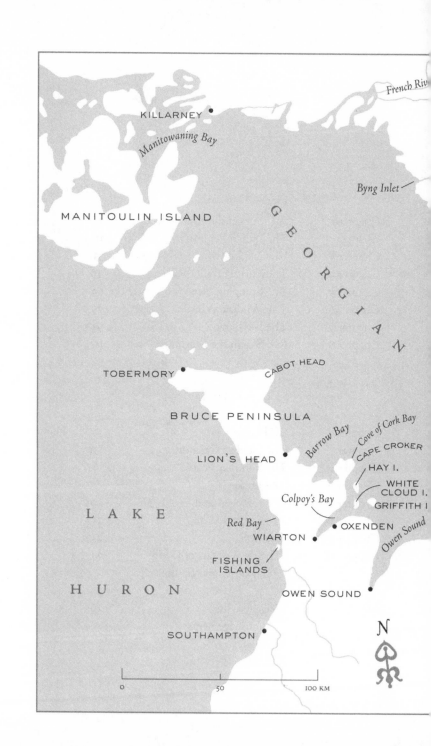

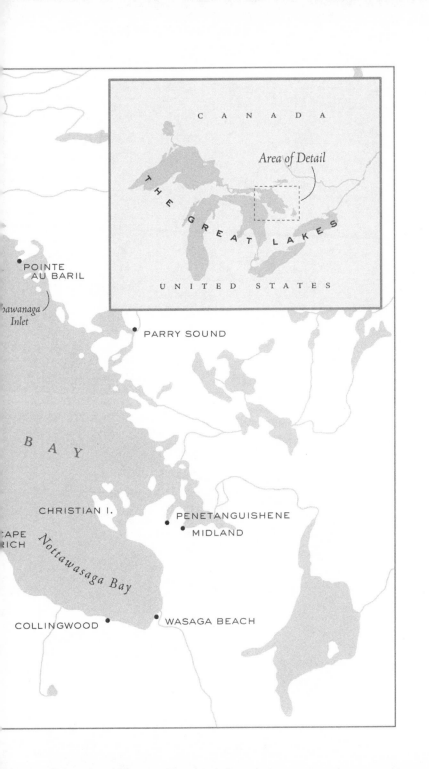

Into the Blue

THE STEAMER JONES

WRECKED

THE SADDEST CALAMITY THAT HAS EVER BEFALLEN WIARTON—WENT DOWN OFF CAPE CROKER AND All Hands were Lost— ABOUT NINETEEN PASSENGERS AND TWELVE OF A CREW—

THE LATTER BELONGED TO WIARTON

Last Thursday morning the steamer Jones, of the Crawford Tug Co., left Owen Sound at 10 o'clock on her regular trip intending to call at Lion's Head and Tobermory. About 1:30 that same day Capt. Chapman saw the boat pass the Cape Croker light, and watched her until she was near the Cove of Corks, and that was the last ever seen of her. When he looked again the Jones had disappeared. Although the weather was not propitious last Thursday Capt. Crawford, who was an old mariner, felt that he could perhaps make Lion's Head, and so left Owen Sound. Nothing was heard of her then for some time and as she had not reported at either Lion's Head or Tobermory, everyone in town became very anxious about her safety. On Sunday this anxiety became very intense, and on Monday and Tuesday, up till the worst fears were confirmed, it was the one topic of conversation.

The Crawford Tug Co. did all in their power to obtain some trace of the boat. They fondly hoped that it was safely at anchor at Cockburn Island or Providence Bay, and they did their best to obtain information but the wires were down on the Manitoulin and this was difficult. On Tuesday, however, the central at Penetang called up John Macaulay, of the Dominion Fish Co., and informed him that the Indians from Christian Island had reported the finding of life boats on the shore with the name J.H. Jones on them, besides some freight consigned to Lion's Head, a barrel of coal oil and parts of the pilot house, caps and life preservers.

This was enough. Everyone then knew that the Jones had foundered and all on board were lost. After she had passed Cape Croker she no doubt encountered a heavy sea, but how the accident occurred is a mere matter of conjecture. It may have been that the captain tried to head her towards land for shelter, the cargo may have shifted, and in a moment the boat went down without, perhaps, one of the passengers or crew having time to put on a life preserver. According to the way the wind was blowing the wreckage would naturally drift to the Christian Islands.

The following were the crew: Capt. J. Crawford; Edward Lennox, 1st mate; George Smith, 2nd mate; Charles Shaw, 1st engineer; Wesley Sadler, 2nd engineer; George McEwen, wheelsman; Willie Ross, wheelsman;——McVittie, fireman; Thomas Simmons, fireman; James Tilley, deck hand; Frank Jackson, cook; Mervin Clark, cook; ——Spears, deckhand, (Colpoys).

As far as can be learned the passengers were: J.T. Donaldson, Manager of the Wolverine Fish Co., Owen Sound; James Fox, Lion's Head; Alex. Lyons and mother Owen Sound; Daniel McIvor, Providence Bay; Marmaduke Vail and son; Frank and George Fellon, Tobermory; and three men being sent by Capt. Graham to Silverwater; Mr. and Mrs. Burley and three children, Shallow Lake; T. M. Wagg, Manitoulin Island; Louis Allen, Owen Sound.

The steamer Jones was the most important boat of the Crawford Tug Co.'s fleet and was valued at $12,000. She was built in 1888 at Goderich for the Dominion Fish Co. and was purchased by the Crawford Tug Co. in 1900. She was thoroughly seaworthy and had passed an inspection last spring, while her hull was inspected last week. The loss is a very heavy one to the company, who are the principal lake carriers at this port.

The crew were all old mariners, thoroughly competent, the boat was equipped with fuel, and the wreck was not due to any want of competency upon the part of any of those on board.

The tug Sandford with a search party left on Tuesday evening for Christian Island. J. Crawford was in charge.

Adapted from The Wiarton Echo, *November 29, 1906*

PART ONE

Steamer "Jones" wrecked in Georgian Bay
Nov. 22nd 1906

In my family's storytelling, the tale of the wreck was only the beginning.

Chapter 1

A PIRATE ON THE FAMILY TREE

FOR AS LONG AS I CAN REMEMBER I have been haunted by shipwrecks. Two in particular colour my fears with rust and slime. One of these boats is a prosaic wooden tug called the *Metamora* that was built in Cleveland in 1864 for service on the Great Lakes. It sank in 1907 about two hundred feet from the slippery pink rock that half a century later would become my father's family island on the east shore of Georgian Bay in Lake Huron. The Wreck, as people in the area know it, sits in

3

about six feet of water in the middle of a wide inlet strewn with treacherous shoals and glacier-rounded islands, smooth in places like a child's skin. On the islands, twisted white pine and dwarf cedar trees have found sustenance in the rocks. They lean and poke at awkward angles, frozen in movement.

The *Metamora* today is little more than a few rusting pieces of machinery that jut out of the waves, yet it has become an icon in the area—a channel marker and a marker of time. We're near The Wreck, we tell people when they ask for directions to our island, knowing they'll understand where we mean. The water certainly is low (or high) on The Wreck, we say to each other every summer, monitoring the spring thaw.

But even more, it has become a measure of our family lore. Remember when Dad dumped us in the dinghy near The Wreck? That friend of yours who wanted to go snorkelling there? Remember that summer when it was so windy you could barely see it rising out of the waves?

When I go swimming off the front dock, I rarely stay in for long because I imagine skeletal fingers tracing a line along the bottom of my foot. I think of the fish who swam near The Wreck and then brushed by me. I won't touch its rusty hull below the waterline and I give it a wide berth when I am forced to go by in a boat. On the rare occasions I am alone on the island I imagine I hear the silver whispers of drowning sailors calling for help.

The *Metamora* was a tug and coal carrier when she sank, but in her early days she had a more fearsome task. Fitted with armour-plating and a cannon, she was commissioned to patrol the waters of Upper Canada for Fenian invaders. In the 1870s, the threat of an Irish invasion gone, her combat gear was removed and she was returned to freight and passenger service. By the day in late September 1907 when she steamed by our island in Shawanaga Inlet near the village of Pointe au Baril, the boat was a confirmed workhorse, plying the channel between Midland and Killarney, towing log booms and handling freight.

Coming up the bay beside Nadeau, one of the larger of the thirty thousand islands that are scattered along this rugged shore, the *Metamora* was towing a boom destined for the mill town of Byng Inlet. Just west of Turning Island, a nearly treeless rock now outfitted with a solar-powered light, the boat hit a shoal, listed and caught fire. Like many wooden boats of her vintage, she quickly burned and sank, coming to rest on the submerged reef that rises and dips from a point off our island.

The crew reportedly made an easy swim of it to the nearby shore. Some of them must have sat on the smooth, undulating rock at our point—the place my family calls Pirate's Cove—breathing heavily, watching the flames gorge on the hull of their ship.

Only the stern section of the 115-foot boat survived the fire, and the rudder, steam engine and propeller remained largely intact. For many years afterward the charred wooden hull rose above the waterline, drawing scavengers and sightseers in wooden rowboats and skiffs. Today, it's only the boiler you can see, a green and black channel marker secured to the rusting metal, and when the water is especially low a set of wooden ribs, looking from a distance like a family of wood ducks floating in a row. Each summer the Coast Guard paints the boiler white, a warning to those who pass by. One year, someone attached three garden gnomes to the metal. They appeared to be marching single file out of the water. Their goofy grins and droopy hats made The Wreck seem benign, silly even, but if you go up close, peer through the undulating water, try to make sense of the garbled remains, it is menacing: a rusted, rotting tangle of metal and wood.

The other shipwreck that lurks on the edge of my imagination is of the same vintage. It, too, sank on Georgian Bay. It was even similar in design and size to the *Metamora*. But the *J. H. Jones* has a more tragic story. All thirty passengers and crew died, drowned in the frigid fall waters of late November 1906. The wreck and the bodies trapped inside were never found.

The story of the *Jones* is also a more personal one for me. My great-grandfather, James Victor Crawford, was the captain. My mother's mother, Eleanor, was the youngest of his six children.

When I was growing up I used to beg my mother to tell me what she knew about this wreck. She would assume the lilting, resonant voice that I recognized from having books read out loud at bedtime. The story of the lost boat seemed to flow from her with the cadence of a familiar song: details were fuzzy, unimportant. Over the years, she perfected her story. I knew when her voice would rise and when it would fall, what would be glossed over, what part would be embellished just a bit differently each time.

Her storytelling always began with the boat: how it was the last trip of a blustery fall season; how the waves were reported to be quivering towers, twenty-five feet high. But we both understood that the tale of the wreck was only the warm-up. That *other* story of loss—the play of hope and despair in the Crawfords' cramped red-brick home as they waited for news of the missing boat; the creak of the door as someone came to tell the captain's wife and children that the *Jones* was definitely lost; the whispers and rumours in the streets and sitting rooms of their small town; the pall cast over the young family; the smells, the cracks and fears and shame—is what interested my mother, and what captivated me. I wanted to hear how the tragedy affected my much-loved grandmother. I wanted to hear about the girl she had been.

Intimidatingly beautiful, with big brown eyes, wavy dark hair and olive skin, my grandmother had a piercing intelligence, the kind that does not suffer fools, sentimentalists or the silliness of small children. She was stylish, self-confident and vain—never without high heels or her trademark costume jewellery. She always lied about her age, though it was hardly necessary since she looked ten years younger than she was at any given time. I feared her slightly but I also adored her, partly because my mother did, and partly also because I knew that her impatience was tempered by a mischievous sense of humour.

My grandmother lived in Montreal and was an unrepentant champion of the city on the St. Lawrence River where she and my grandfather, Paul Smith, raised their two daughters—my mother, Erica, and her older sister, Paula. I grew up thinking that Montreal was the epitome of sophistication and glamour and that my grandmother and the city were inseparable.

She inspired respect in those who knew her, but also friendship, and when she died in 1983 she was mourned by a legion of friends and acquaintances she knew through my grandfather's work as a lawyer, city councillor and sportsman as well as through her own volunteer commitments. I always felt that at least some of the admiration she commanded must have been because of the astounding height of the hair that she piled on top of her head, then twisted into an exotic knot. Until she passed away in her late seventies, she dyed it a deep, warm brown.

I saw her only once with her hair undone. She was brushing it in the bedroom of her townhouse in Montreal and I happened to walk by the open door. Her hair was flat against her head and hung limply almost to her waist. I could see the grey roots, which were usually hidden by a French roll. I was shocked to see her looking so shrunken and old, like a witch.

I don't think my grandmother saw me that day and I never mentioned it to her. In fact, I never told anyone I'd seen her like that. She was always so pulled together, so self-assured and elegant, that to say I had seen her looking less than beautiful, even frightening, felt like a betrayal.

And yet it was the beginning of my understanding that everything was not entirely as it seemed. If my grandmother was not always beautiful, she might not be the other things I had believed about her. The incident opened the door for me to see that my mother's story had missing pieces.

Wiarton, Ontario, the tiny lakeside town on the Bruce Peninsula where my grandmother grew up and where most of the *Jones*'s crew made their home, had always appeared in my mother's stories as a kind of secondary character. Squatting near the base of the peninsula at the head of a long bay, the bustling hamlet was carved out of the wilderness, an upstart challenger to bigger, more southerly ports for the lucrative Georgian Bay shipping trade. The way my mother described it, Wiarton was a frontier community of lumber barons and shopkeepers, poor farmers and self-righteous church ladies. My grandmother ran away from it as soon as she could.

It's a southern Ontario landscape that was familiar to me despite the gap of two generations. I'd spent summers on Georgian Bay and grew up not far inland, in a town that experienced many of the same cycles of boom and bust that Wiarton did. I had also left my small town as soon as I was able. Yet even with this intimate knowledge of the landscape and my mother's evocative telling, I still found it difficult to picture my grandmother in that place.

For one thing, she never spoke of it. And we had virtually no contact with her family who still lived in the area; I only visited Wiarton once when I was very small. My grandmother had cut herself off from her relatives and the place where she spent her first eighteen years. When she died, many of her longtime friends knew nothing of her life before she moved to Montreal. My grandmother had reinvented herself.

As I got older and realized for myself the effort involved in her transformation from the impoverished daughter of a drowned shipping captain to the well-heeled Montreal matron I knew, I wanted more than ever to fill in the gaps. I asked more questions and heard that she had once thought she would be a poet or a journalist. I learned, shockingly, of a mysterious first marriage and the child she had been forced to abandon.

About ten years after she died, I received a package in the mail from my aunt Paula in Montreal. I was living in Toronto by then, struggling to write fiction and magazine articles while working as a copy editor at a local magazine. I might have been asking my mother and aunt more questions about the family story, but I remember thinking that the package arrived out of the blue, even as something of a directive. In a note that accompanied it, my aunt, who is a painter, wrote that she hoped that "as a writer," I might enjoy some of my grandmother's poetry and letters.

I'd never seen Eleanor's writing before, though knowing of her literary ambitions had made my own urge to write seem less odd and unattainable. I remembered that she had taken a special interest in the fairy tales I wrote as a child and kindly tucked away my teenage melodramas about misunderstood girls who died too young. I think my family thought that by choosing to pursue writing and editing, I was following in her footsteps.

I opened the package but didn't read the poems right away. I worried that I would find the writing old-fashioned or hackneyed, that the woman I had admired so much—whose literary heir I was supposed to be—had been a lousy poet.

When I did finally dig into my grandmother's writing, I read it all in one sitting. Most of the pieces were written when she was a teenager and in her early twenties, with a few composed later on. Some were carefully typed out, while others were written on lined paper in a headlong script, words violently scratched out and replaced. Several of the poems seemed inspired by Victorian verse, overstuffed with notions of Beauty, Art, Ecstasy and Pain; but there were others of a more modern bent, daring to use the first person, to speak plainly. All of them had an autobiographical tone, a sense of urgency, as if writing was the only way to release her thoughts into the world. There were a couple of angry poems about her aunt Susie, who raised her when her sick mother could no longer do so. She called one piece "Failure," another "Frustration."

The writing was uneven, as you might expect from pieces that span several decades, but there were also flashes of insight and vivid, deeply imagined turns of phrase. Most importantly, I found that my grandmother's hurts, loves and disappointments seeped like fresh ink from the page, and I began to be able to imagine her, the young woman whose friend admonished in an unsigned letter: "Please do not stagnate. . . . I know from your paroxysmal mental states of extreme joy and melancholia that you are capable to see byond [*sic*] and feel byond the mere animate being. . . ." I was thrust back to my own self-conscious adolescence when I read her lament: "Why can't I always seem/ Complete and beautiful and glad?"

By the time I reached the final poems I had a better sense of the young woman she had once been, but I was not much further along in understanding what had made her reject this earlier life and reinvent herself. She wrote of her struggle to leave Wiarton behind, but not why she had to. She described an uneasiness with her family's expectations and fear of her own limitations, but that, of course, is a common teenage refrain. None of it seemed like enough to spur a wholesale rejection of her past.

But then, near the end of the package, a poem simply called "Villanelle" forced me to look at it all—everything I'd read and heard—in a new light.

I have an aunt as godly as can be.
She says I'm a most unprincipled miss
But I have a pirate on my family tree.

I break men's hearts so carelessly
Never give more than the littlest kiss
I have an aunt as godly as can be

She says I'm a devil, stealing with glee
Some other nicer girl's chance of bliss
But I have a pirate on my family tree

He was bad so splendidly
I've heard my grandpa reminisce
I have an aunt as godly as can be.

She says I'm sunk in iniquity
She says I'll end in hell's abyss
But I have a pirate on my family tree.

Dear Auntie's heaven is closed to me
There's no one there that I will miss
I have an aunt as godly as can be
But I have a pirate on my family tree.

There was the cruel aunt and the spirited young girl who tries to go her own way. It was the pirate part that was new to me.

I'd like to say I understood that day that her father, James Victor Crawford, the owner and master of the ill-fated *J. H. Jones*, was the pirate. I'd like to say that the influence of the wreck on her life was apparent to me from that moment on. But the truth is, I didn't understand at all.

It took several years of bumbling, digging in newspaper archives and talking to relatives and friends my grandmother hadn't spoken to since she left Wiarton at eighteen to understand that her father's absence was a defining presence in my grandmother's life. It took me that long to see that I'd missed something important when I'd impatiently skipped over the story of the *Jones* and her father's death to hear the details of her girlhood. To really know my grandmother, to comprehend the debt I owed to her, I realized that I would have to get to know this man and his boat. I would have to excavate the story of the *Jones*.

Two local history booklets have been written about the tragedy; diving books name it among the hundred most sought-after shipwrecks in the Great Lakes. There are numerous newspaper accounts from the time of the wreck, and even today articles pop up each fall in the local paper. In the early days, especially, the newspapers printed extraordinary details about the lives of the passengers and crew, about the debris that washed up more than a hundred miles east of where the boat was last sighted. I found poems written by family members of the victims and a sea shanty composed to commemorate its loss. I even discovered a chair with the words "*J. H. Jones*" stencilled on the back, tucked deep in the bowels of an Owen Sound museum.

My grandmother's family history was also relatively straightforward to track down. The *Wiarton Echo*, the local newspaper, found it worthwhile to include much unlikely minutiae about the lives of the Crawford clan ("Captain J. V. Crawford's little girl, who is just old enough to run about, had the misfortune to come in contest with the hot stove. The little thing placed both hands on the stove and was very badly burnt, but the wounds are now healing nicely"). The rising fortunes of the Crawford Tug Company, which my great-grandfather owned with his two older brothers, were monitored each week in the newspaper as it grew from one tug to a fleet of seven steamers and several smaller boats. Within the family, pictures, books, wills, deeds and photographs have survived a century of careful tending.

But this excavation also led me places I never imagined going. I found myself deep inside the history of Georgian Bay—this lake that formed everyone who formed me. I got to know the people of late-nineteenth and early-twentieth century Wiarton, their worries and preoccupations, their successes and disappointments. I read the shipping news of the 1880s and 1890s, when reports of burned and scuttled steamboats were surprisingly commonplace. I discovered that although Georgian Bay is now the happy summer playground of cottagers and daytrippers, it was once the booming heart of an emerging nation's economy. The emanations of this lost world are still everywhere on the bay. I am reminded of this each time I stand near Pirate's Cove at our cottage and see the water smashing against the rusting boiler of that other wreck, the *Metamora*.

I also discovered the limitations of the artifacts and documents, of the histories written about the region. Stories I read about the *Jones* often contradicted one another: official versions are edited and revised—for posterity, for pride, for shame—and bear only passing resemblance to the memories handed down the generations in my family. Rumours have gained the status of truth; facts are obscured by time, distance and those who tell the story. The artifacts are also clouded by the vast and varied needs of those who possess them. I decided that the only way I could solve the enigma of my grandmother and her father's legacy was to grasp at the fragments I could define, to distill the stories, strain them through the sieve of hindsight. I would have to use what facts I could find and imagine the rest.

ॐ

November 22, 1906, 1 p.m., Owen Sound, Georgian Bay

Jim Crawford strokes the soft whiskers of his moustache with one hand, and grips the door frame of the wheelhouse with the other. The dull light of midday makes the long fingers of land on either side of the *Jones* look naked and sharp. The sky is low and there are reports of big waves out in the open, but the storm should be passing. Jim tugs his hat down over his ears and goes back inside.

Willie Ross is at the helm. He's a good man. He's been grumbling a bit this morning, saying he wishes he was home, warm in front of the stove, but he'll get over it. He always does.

Through the two narrow windows, Jim can see an expanse of open water in front of them, waves melting into the horizon in the distance, the curve of Coffin Hill to the east. Reaching the mouth of the bay, big, frothy whitecaps greet the steamer, a thin mist rising from the crash of the waves. Jim buttons his oilskin up tightly.

It's the same every fall. A chill sets in around mid-month. There are sudden blinding snow squalls, and heavy seas wipe out landmarks and lights. The magnetic compass spins around like a trapped snake. It's nothing he hasn't seen before but, still, the men are edgy, ready to finish for the season. That morning at the docks he caught the new assistant cook talking nonsense about the old Wiarton boat, the *Jane Miller*, wrecked near Griffith Island. The boy told anyone who'd listen that today is the twenty-fifth anniversary of its foundering. All the old sailors know it already, of course. They don't need reason to be more superstitious. They don't need reminding of the wrecked boat, the twenty-five local people drowned. One pair of oars, a broken flagstaff, a fire-bucket rack and five cloth caps—a precise inventory—washed up on nearby White Cloud Island.

Local fishermen drag out the story every time they have a bad day on the water and say the *Miller* is a ghost ship haunting the mouth of Colpoy's Bay, marking her tomb with oily black bubbles that rise to the surface, discolouring the water.

Jim told the boy it would be his first and last trip if he didn't keep his big jaw shut and get to work. The young man trudged away with his head down, dragging a huge bag of potatoes along the dock behind him.

The sky has begun to turn a leaden grey, but Jim can still make out the outline of Griffith Island's southeastern shore. He's so familiar with the passage he can catalogue the puzzle of big flat rocks with his eyes, mentally tracing the shoreline, remembering where the water drops off suddenly, where, if you know the waves and winds, it is possible to land a small boat. He's taken many trips there on the *Jones* and countless other boats. He thinks sometimes that he knows the shore and waters of Georgian Bay better than he knows his own family.

With open water to starboard and the thickly wooded island to port, the boat steams ahead steadily. As Jim and Willie Ross spot the Griffith Island lighthouse, snow starts to beat a furious tattoo against the wooden deck.

Jim sends for first mate Ed Lennox to make sure the passengers stay inside. The rollers might make them feel green, but they'll have to sit tight in the small cabins if they don't want to catch their deaths.

Out the window, Jim and Willie can see the sky lowering like a stage curtain. If it wasn't for the whitecaps, they couldn't tell the air from the seething water. Waves begin to crash over the *Jones*'s bow.

*It wasn't long after Jim Crawford left the family farm that he got
a taste of rough-and-tumble life on the Wiarton docks.*

Chapter 2

THE INDIAN PENINSULA

ON A MAP, the Bruce Peninsula looks like a knife, its jagged shore the double-sided blade slicing Lake Huron in two. Shaped from dolomite limestone, the narrow, crooked shaft of land sixty miles long is part of an ancient rock shelf that begins along the west and northern shore of Lake Michigan and heads southeast. Below the Bruce you can track the shale-like white rock in the highlands of southern Ontario down to the eroding sill of Niagara Falls.

The peninsula marks the western boundary of Georgian Bay, a fist of fresh water often called the sixth Great Lake. Located near the exact centre of continental North America, the bay gets hit by weather from every direction. Air masses from the Arctic, Pacific and Atlantic Oceans, as well as the Gulf of Mexico and western North America converge there. The result is unpredictable weather all year round. In the windswept trees and smooth rocks, in the jagged cliffs and beaches, you can see the way the weather has carved the land.

The Bruce shore, with Wiarton near its bottom, is a wall of stone—sharp grey cliffs rising from the water, looming and impressive. The southern basin around the town of Wasaga Beach is low-lying and fertile, the place where glaciers deposited sand stretching far into the bay. The eastern coast, where my family's island is located, is part of the Canadian Shield, an enormous band of Precambrian rock shredded and worn by time. Some of the thirty thousand islands along this shore are large, others the size of a small car. Many are unpopulated. The farther northwest you move along this side of the bay, the more wild and desolate the land appears, until the islands seem more like a moonscape than a place where people and plants could thrive. The northwestern border of Georgian Bay is guarded by Manitoulin Island, the largest freshwater island in the world and part of the same limestone corridor that makes up the Bruce Peninsula. The Ojibway people say that Gitchi Manitou, the Great Spirit, once inhabited its pretty coves and tree-lined bluffs.

While each shore has its own unique ecology and geology, the land around Georgian Bay is linked by the water it shares. *La Mer Douce* (the sweetwater sea)—as Samuel de Champlain, the governor of New France and the first European to write about exploration in the area, called it—is a natural thoroughfare, a conduit of flora, fauna, people and ideas.

For hundreds of years, the site of the future town of Wiarton at the head of Colpoy's Bay was an entry point to that thoroughfare, a dense cedar swamp at the terminus of an eight-mile portage. The peninsula is narrowest there, and the overland route from Lake Huron allowed Native trappers and fishermen to avoid making the long and treacherous pass by water around the top of the peninsula, through the gap into Georgian Bay and the trading routes on the northeast shore.

By 1854, the Saugeen and Nawash Ojibway—who had lived in the area for generations, fishing and hunting —were so sick and their populations so depleted by war and European diseases that they were persuaded by the Crown, anxious to open more land to white settlers, to "extinguish" their title to the land. In exchange, they were given four small tracts on the peninsula and the under-standing that twice a year "so long as there were Indians left to represent the tribe," they would receive payments from the interest on the sale of their lands.

Surveyed by the government in 1855, the village of Wiarton wasn't settled by European immigrants until the late 1860s when the Department of Indian Affairs put up money to build a wharf. Soon, a steamer from Owen Sound was making a trip each day to the marshy little clearing at the head of deep and unobstructed Colpoy's Bay. The new settlers, however, were greeted by little more than hordes of mosquitoes and flocks of wild pigeon so thick that young boys batted them out of the air with clubs and snagged them with fishing nets.

Twelve-year-old James Victor Crawford, his six siblings and widowed father, Samuel Crawford Sr., arrived in the region, known then as the Saugeen or Indian Peninsula, in 1867. Paying the Department of Indian Affairs $300, Samuel Sr., a veterinary surgeon and native of county Donegal, Ireland, bought a parcel of land near the bur-geoning village of Oxenden about three miles east of Wiarton. A crossroads on the south shore of Colpoy's Bay, Oxenden was thought to have the potential to become the principal village in the area: a commercial hub, a port of call. By the time the Crawfords arrived in the hardscrabble hamlet in the township of Keppel, there was already a small brown church deep in the wildwood, a school, a store and the distinction of a post office. A blacksmith and wagon shop was set up near the old Ojibway chief's house close to the water. Farms were being carved from the wilderness farther inland. There would be lots of work for someone with veterinary skills.

Samuel Sr. was ambitious for his family. He and his late wife had hoped their boys would be educated, as he had been at the University of Dublin before emigrating in the 1840s. But formal education was unlikely with the closest high school a full day's journey over corduroy roads, so he made certain the children had other opportu-nities. Samuel Jr., the eldest son, would learn veterinary medicine at his side. And Middleton, christened with his mother's maiden name, had uncanny mechanical smarts. He could build anything, fix anything. Samuel Sr. offered him a small amount of money to start a business. He'd do well in such a self-made place.

The younger boys, Jim, William and John Thomas (whose friends called him Jack), helped clear the family's boulder-strewn land for farming while the two girls, Jennie and Margaret, looked after the Crawfords' small homestead. None of it was easy. The township wasn't known as "rocky Keppel" for nothing.

There was comfort in the fact that others were in the same position. Protestant Scots and Irish like the Crawfords were numerous in Keppel. They stuck together, helped one another out. It didn't take long for some of the men to organize building a small hall near the cemetery to hold Orange Lodge meetings.

An ardent Orangeman, Samuel Sr. held the post of Deputy District Master for many years, relishing his leading role in the annual July parade—the Glorious 12th. The girls would wear starched white dresses, the boys their best coats. There would be music and banners, the band playing "Protestant Boys" and "Croppies Lie Down." Celebrating a war victory 250 years and a continent away, the whole village would trail behind a man dressed as King Billy astride a big grey horse festooned with pompoms and paper flowers. Once the parade was finished, the men would bring out their homemade whisky. The singers would grow bolder; the merrymakers merrier. The Glorious 12th often ended in a fight.

Life in Oxenden was rough-and-tumble much of the time. Timber operations were flourishing by the 1870s and the annual influx of young men from the south and the east set a tone of transience and lawlessness. A band of thieves known as the "Keppel Robbers" tormented the whole peninsula until the Wiarton justice of the peace brought their spree to an end. And the Oxenden cemetery, perched on top of a gentle rise not far from the Crawford farm, was said to possess the remains of seven murder victims whose killers were never brought to justice.

Loggers had started to arrive on the peninsula not long after the Crawford family. Licences to cut the region's forests had been available since the treaty with the Ojibway in the 1850s, but large-scale operators took another decade to recognize the area's potential. By then, red pine and spruce, rock elm and hemlock were being cut and rafted away to be sold in the south. But it was the stands of big white pine in the northern reaches of the peninsula that would prove to be the most desirable.

As activity in the forests grew, the gap between the interests of the logging operations and those of the early landholders became more and more pronounced. The settlers complained that timber licence-holders like the Cook Brothers of Barrie functioned above the law, in cahoots with politicians in faraway Ottawa. The loggers themselves were rowdy and careless. When they mistakenly felled substandard trees, they'd simply leave them to rot in the fields of mud, stumps and slash—ideal conditions for a forest fire. But it was for the Department of Indian Affairs, which sold both the timber licences and land rights, that the landowners reserved particular vitriol. It hadn't taken long for settlers to figure out that title to the land didn't include ownership of the trees. Until these families—struggling just to put food on the table, let alone make enough money to pay their debt—paid off the full purchase price of their property, they didn't have the right to cut their own trees. They were allowed to fell those necessary to erect farm buildings, but the rest belonged to the lumber company with a timber licence for the area.

This policy made it so hard to make a go of settlement on the peninsula that a great number of the early pioneers abandoned their land and left the area. Once the trees had been harvested, the settlers who stayed discovered the soil underneath was patchy and thin, in many cases unfarmable.

But even those fortunate pioneers who weren't affected by the Department of Indian Affairs' policy found their lives inextricably tied to the lumber trade. It was inescapable. Sawmills were popping up all over the area— eight at the lower end of Colpoy's Bay alone, and another thirty smaller mills up and down the peninsula. Profits from the clearing of the forests started a boom. When the Grand Trunk Railway finally arrived in Wiarton in 1882, the peninsula's reliance on lumber was sealed.

It was pouring rain on the August day that the train pulled into the village for the first time. But the five thousand spectators who had flooded into Wiarton from as far away as Stratford were too roused by patriotic speeches and anticipation to care about the weather. Flags and streamers flew from all the businesses and homes along the main street, and four different arches made of spruce and pine boughs were arranged overtop the muddy road. Local businessmen had argued for days about what to write on their arch. They finally agreed on the nonpartisan but sufficiently enthusiastic "The Merchants hail the advent of the Iron Steed." People swarmed the village, clambering onto the limestone cliffs to get a better view of the train and the festivities. No longer would there be any question about scrappy Oxenden being the primary port on Colpoy's Bay. With a railroad connection to the rest of the province, Wiarton had usurped all contenders. It was a backwoods hamlet no more.

That summer, twenty-five carloads of lumber and wood products were shipped out of the village every day. Sometimes it would take three locomotives to pull the heavily laden cars up the steep hill from the sawmills. Children would run alongside, yelling and pumping their arms, hoping for a yank on the steam whistle. Wiarton's beach was littered with sawdust, its sawmills were churning out lumber and squared timber destined for England, the U.S. and the rest of Canada. The Ojibway had once called Colpoy's Bay Wahshushweequaid—the bay of muskrats—but by the mid-1880s it had become more surely the bay of log booms.

Wiartonians dared to think that their village would outstrip larger towns nearby like Collingwood, Midland and Owen Sound as the most important port on Georgian Bay. The harbour was deep and free of shoals; the steep escarpment running along the northern edge of the bay protected the docks and the village from wind and weather. "That Wiarton is destined at no far future date to become a place of considerable importance, is obvious to anyone who has given the matter any serious reflection," the new village newspaper, the *Wiarton Echo*, informed its readers.

Samuel Sr.'s son Middleton agreed. He'd left the family farm to move to the village several years before the railroad arrived. He built Wiarton's first steam-powered grist and flour mill in the early 1880s right on the beach south of the main dock. The business was so promising he tried to convince his younger brothers, still working the family farm, to join him.

The Crawford farm had taken several years of hard labour just to get going. The stumps had to be cleared, then the brothers had to dig out stones and boulders and pile them in mid-field clumps and fencelines marking the edge of their property. Jack had become known for his strength. People said he was built like an ox and could handle logs or rocks like a man twice his size. All his life, people remembered the way he broke and trained a frisky grey horse named Dunk belonging to the Scot who people in the area knew as the Laird O' Keppel. Still, Jack was glad to get away from farming; he was the first to join his brother at the mill.

By the fall of 1882, not long after the arrival of the first Grand Trunk rail car, the brothers were doing so well that they decided to expand their operation and purchase a tugboat. The *Jennie Harper* would be used to carry grain and flour, but would also be available for towing and hauling other people's goods.

When his brothers asked him, young Jim Crawford also left the farm. He would take on the responsibility of master of the *Jennie Harper*. He hadn't much experience on the water, just fishing in a little skiff with his brothers and friends, but such limited training wasn't uncommon for sailors at the time. Like every other boy growing up on Georgian Bay, Jim had been raised on stories about the famed steamboat captains of Collingwood and Midland. He'd heard about the races they had and the chances they took. Still, nothing could have prepared him for his first season on the water.

It wasn't long after Jim took over the *Jennie Harper* that he had a taste of how rough it could get on the Wiarton docks. It was late fall, the ice nearly in, and Jim was loading the *Harper* for a final delivery up the peninsula, when Captain C. W. Menton barrelled into the village claiming that the boat belonged to him. He angrily demanded Jim turn it over—or else. A small man, but imposing when he wanted to be, Jim Crawford stepped down onto the dock. "Or else," he said, taking up the challenge. Infuriated, Captain Menton started swinging at him. When John Ashcroft, a well-known businessman in the village, stepped in to stop the fight, Menton lunged at him as well. It became a brawl. Dragged in front of the local magistrate, Captain Menton was quickly convicted on two counts of assault and fined $1.00 plus costs.

And if such a welcome into the sailing fraternity weren't enough to make a farmer like Jim Crawford doubt his new profession, a series of tragic fires and wrecks made 1882 one of the worst years in the recorded history of shipping on Georgian Bay. With several hundred people drowned and hundreds of thousands of dollars' worth of boats and cargo sunk to the bottom of the lake, a chill passed through the towns and villages that circled the bay. It was clear then if it hadn't been before: the water would give, but it would also take away.

⁂

April 9, 1883, Wiarton harbour

Jim likes to watch the ice melt. Starting at the end of March he makes a point of walking down to the docks each day, even if he has no business there. The thaw always starts in the shallow areas close to shore, slabs of ice pulling away from the rocks and sand to reveal water like an eager puppy lapping at the rock. Day by day it shrinks back, pinging and snapping as it melts. Then dark patches appear, cracks like fault lines criss-crossing Colpoy's Bay, the water black against the snow-covered ice.

Sometimes he wakes up after a windy night and the bay is entirely clear. Other times the retreat of the ice is slow and methodical, a reluctant inch at a time, the sound of ice and water smashing together like a rushing spring waterfall. The men in town bet cigars and chewing tobacco, wagering on the day of the opening of navigation.

This morning the bay is still locked tight but the harbour is beginning to wake up. There are sailors scrubbing the whitework on the boats in dry dock, stevedores stacking supplies ready for the first steamer brave enough to venture out. But the young men loitering around the docks are the most obvious sign the long siege of winter is lifting. Fresh from working someone else's timber limits, they're thin and ruddy-faced, smelling of burning wood and tobacco, flush with a winter's wage in their pockets.

Jim has only been a captain for one season but he already knows what the old-timers mean when they talk about the longing they feel after the winter layaway. You crave the wind and sun on your skin, the thrum of the engine beneath your feet. You spend each night dreaming of riding the swells on the open bay. During the day, it pokes you in the gut when you're thinking about other things.

Looking out at the bay, Jim pats down the bushy bits at the front of his moustache, then runs one finger along to the side and twirls the end between his thumb and forefinger. It's a habit of his. His older brother Jack likes to tease him about it, says his ritual makes him look like a dandy. But it's Jack and Middleton who love the tailor-made suits. They're the businessmen of the family. Jack is part of every new venture that happens in the village—fancies himself something of a capitalist.

The sight of the barren, purple-tinged islands at the mouth of the bay reminds Jim of the promise he made to himself at the close of last season. He decided then that, though it might be difficult, he would continue on the water. He'd never go back to farming the thin, unwilling soil of the family homestead. He might even buy his own boat someday. In the enthusiasm and bravado of those last trips before the ice came in, it had seemed like a reasonable goal, the sort of thing that any right-thinking young man might aspire to. Now, blunted by a long winter of making do with odd jobs at the flour mill and the goodwill of his brothers, it feels like a pipe dream.

Jim hears a loud crack. The dock seems to shake slightly in the echo. The ice is breaking up. It won't be long now before the wind takes it sailing to the north shore.

He steps off the wharf onto the beach. It's marshy and wet, covered in wood chips and sawdust from the nearby mill. Snow lingers in the shadows in dark, sooty patches. Walking southward, he can feel a change in the wind. Even through the pulpy smell of the sawmills, there's the distinct scent of green: new weather is blowing in.

The men on the docks say he has a weather eye. But he can feel it in his bones and nose as well as his eyes. It's almost like he was born on the water, not some blighted farm. Jim tells the others it's just because he trusts his instincts. The glass and his gut. But he can't pretend it doesn't please him that the other sailors have noticed.

He undoes the buttons of his jacket and lets the damp spring wind blow it open. It tears at his linen shirt underneath. He smiles, pulling at the ends of his moustache again. He breathes the Georgian Bay air deep into his lungs and heads back to the village.

Of all the many boosters in Wiarton in the early years, Albert Munroe Tyson was one of the most vociferous. The lakeside village had been good to him.

Chapter 3

SAWDUST TOWN

THE LUMBER INDUSTRY brought noisy prosperity to Wiarton. Accommodation was available at any of five hotels, and young men looking for girls to ogle could go to five separate church services on Sunday if they chose. Grand Victorian homes began to rise up on the hill leading south and the village stores sold handsome ready-made suits, dresses and shoes straight from Orangeville, Toronto and Montreal. The population nearly tripled in the decade between 1881 and 1891.

And yet, Wiarton was still in the heart of the wilderness. Bears were a common sight around town and lynx were known to steal farmers' sheep. Hogs and cows ran freely through the streets (although, as the editor of the *Echo* reminded readers, letting livestock loose in the village was against local bylaws).

Down by the water, the beach was so coated with detritus from the sawmills, people began to call Wiarton Sawdust Town. The bay was invariably full of logs left drifting until the mills were ready to process them. Teenage boys liked to strip naked and race on the rolling timbers trapped in the harbour, skipping and jumping, teasing the water with their toes.

But the booms could also be dangerous. The largest ones covered up to twenty-five acres and needed three tugs to pull them. Even the smaller booms moved at glacial speeds, knocking down everything in their path. Other sailors hated them because a giant mass of rolling logs passing through a narrow area would often force larger boats aground. Or a boom might jam a main channel and steamers and their crews would have to sit in harbour, waiting—sometimes for days—while the log rafts were cleared. And out in fog or the disorienting darkness of open water, the badly marked and unruly booms sometimes rammed unsuspecting steamers.

The demand for timber, however, was insatiable. While the rest of the province staggered through a recession for much of the late nineteenth century, the Bruce Peninsula (as it had become known, for James Bruce, governor of Canada in the 1850s) prospered.

Around the Wiarton docks, steamboats and tugs, schooners and Collingwood skiffs jostled for space. The acrid smell of burning coal and woodsmoke mingled with the damp odour emerging from the fish house on the north shore.

The fishing industry was second only to lumber as an economic force in the region. The plentiful whitefish in Lake Huron and Georgian Bay had become the stuff of legend. Stories were passed from village to village about a man who bought a wool suit, a gallon of whisky and a milk cow with the money from selling just one sturgeon. Although the large-scale companies were gaining control of the market, even small-time fishermen could make a decent living—as long as their linen nets didn't tear or disappear and the weather held. They had to be excellent sailors, able to negotiate the Minotaur's maze of islands and shoals in their small sailing boats.

In the early 1880s, fishing companies began to build stations around the bay, hiring the local fishermen and bringing in others. It wasn't an easy life holed up in isolated shanties built on rock, subject to the whims of the fickle bay. But some of the men would bring their wives and children up for a visit, occasionally for the whole season. And if they were lucky, a travelling fiddler would stop by once or twice a summer. There'd be dances then, heavy shoes beating a rhythm on rough floors, couples performing cotillions and quadrilles. On the bigger islands, cows might be imported and put to pasture; and raspberry and whortleberry, haws, bilberries, pin cherries and strawberries were plentiful if you knew where to look. At least once a week the companies would send their steamboats to pick up the fish packed in boxes of ice to be transported to the railway heads bound for New York, Detroit and Philadelphia.

The Wiarton fish house was opened by two Goderich-based businessmen in 1882 to coincide with the arrival of the railway. But within a few years an American firm called the Buffalo Fish Company had bought it out. It didn't take long for the fish house to become one of the most important employers in Wiarton, its operations growing to include a processing plant, ice houses, steamboats and smaller tenders.

When Middleton and Jack Crawford bought the *Jennie Harper* for the flour mill, they made certain the manager at Buffalo Fish understood that the boat was also available for hire.

If it weren't for the fish company, in fact, Middleton's decision to leave Wiarton and close the flour mill might have been the end of the Crawford brothers' foray into shipping. But after the mill stopped work in 1884, the fish house (and other local merchants, who hired out the Crawford tug for hauling and towing) kept Jim and Jack in business.

By 1887, the brothers actually needed a bigger boat to accommodate the increased demand for their services. That spring, they traded the *Jennie Harper* to a Meaford captain for the larger and more powerful tug *Agnes*.

It was April, and the ice had just gone out when Jim Crawford brought the *Agnes* into Wiarton on its inaugural voyage. According to Great Lakes tradition, the village merchants gave him a silk top hat for bringing the first boat of the season into harbour. The businessmen and villagers who gathered on the dock also took it upon themselves to present the homegrown captain with a less common token of their esteem: a small silk handkerchief.

That year the *Agnes* and Captain Jim took on some jobs towing log booms but did much of their work for the

Buffalo Fish Company. The shrewd and knowledgeable manager, John Macaulay, was just a bit younger than Jim and they became friends.

Born to a family of Scottish anglers and mariners who had settled on Lake Huron in the town of Southampton, Macaulay started fishing at thirteen when he dropped out of school to help his father and uncles. Later, he worked on Manitoulin Island and spent four years setting up a Buffalo Fish Company station on the Bustard Islands in eastern Georgian Bay. By the time he arrived in Wiarton, Macaulay was only in his twenties but already an old hand.

Business was so vigorous that in 1887 the Buffalo Fish Company commissioned the construction of a brand-new vessel to be based out of Wiarton. The following spring, the *J. H. Jones*, named for the company's Buffalo-based president, was launched to great fanfare. The 107-foot steam tug was the effort of renowned Goderich ship-wright Billy Marlton. When the *Jones* pulled into Wiarton harbour for the first time, a cargo of fish in her hold, local sailors proclaimed she rode on the water as lightly as a duck. "She is new throughout," noted the *Echo*, "the best material has been used in her build, and no expense has been spared in making her a first class boat both for speed and seaworthiness."

That summer, people in Wiarton bragged that the *Jones* was one of the fastest vessels around. Her reputation was confirmed one day in August when she raced the S.S. *Baltic* down fifteen miles of Colpoy's Bay, both boats' funnels spewing black clouds into the humid sky. When the vessels reached the government docks, people watching from the Wiarton shore swore that the *Jones* was slightly ahead of the much larger steamer.

The Crawford brothers didn't expect to compete with the big shipping companies and American-owned enterprises like Buffalo Fish. They had to count on the promise that there was enough towing and hauling to keep both company boats and privately owned tugs like the *Agnes* in work. The brothers put in long hours just to keep up. Jack had acquired a reputation as an astute businessman. He looked after the books and took care of seeking out new work. Jim was responsible for all things related to the boat. Middleton, too, remained involved, though he had moved south of the border.

Tinkering for years on various inventions, Middleton made his fortune in 1888 when he sold the patent for a machine he designed that cleaned cotton seeds. A few years later, he came up with another device, this one to separate gold from rock. A company in the U.S. bought the machine and the patent for $500,000 in cash, plus other benefits. Middleton became a very rich man, with homes in England, New York and Monte Carlo. In Wiarton they said he was the next best thing to Edison. He remained a partner in his brothers' shipping interests, helping out when they needed capital.

On the home front, things did not run so smoothly for the Crawfords. Tragedy shook the family all through the 1880s. First it was the youngest Crawford sibling, Jennie, who died when she was thirty years old in 1882. Then Jack's wife, Alice Ford, passed away in 1885, leaving him with two small children to care for. Samuel Sr. died in the summer of 1886. And in February 1887, Jim's bride, Jennie Finch, died of a kidney ailment at only twenty-seven years of age. People in the village were kind to the Crawfords, leaving pies and hot meals at the door of Jack's house in the village. Margaret Crawford, who'd never married, moved in to look after Jack's son and daughter. Jack wasn't interested in remarrying (he would live with his sister for the rest of his life), but Jim made it known that he still wanted to have children, a wife, a home of his own.

It was little more than a year later that he began to notice Lillie Tyson, whose family lived next door to Jack. He frequently dealt with her father, Albert, at the village customs house. She'd grown up to be a rather striking girl, a teacher. She'd been away from home for a few years and it gave her a confidence that he liked. When Lillie returned to Wiarton for good after attending the Toronto Normal School, Jim spent as much time as possible on the Tysons' wide front porch.

Of all the many boosters in Wiarton in the early days, Albert Munroe Tyson was probably one of the most vociferous. As the village's third reeve and customs officer, and later, town treasurer and county commissioner, he considered it his job to promote the pleasures and promise of the lakeside burg. It had been good to him.

Albert was born in Waterloo County of German Mennonite stock. His father was the first of the large Tyson clan to move north from Pennsylvania, abandoning his religion once he arrived. When Albert met and married Elizabeth Kelly, of county Wicklow, Ireland, they migrated around the southern part of Ontario for several years before packing up their three children and heading north to the newly opened Indian Peninsula.

The Tysons arrived in Keppel in 1874, seven years after the Crawfords made the same arduous journey on the muddy and rutted Garafraxa Road. Bess (as Albert called her) was pregnant with their fourth child; their eldest, Lillie Elizabeth, was only seven years old. It was a long trip with young children, bumping along with all their worldly goods on wagons and horseback, but the Tysons were hopeful. They'd heard good things about the peninsula. People said fish were abundant in the lake and a man with a head on his shoulders could make his fortune there. An avid outdoorsman with a mind for business, Albert must have thought he was headed to the promised land.

For several years, the Tyson family worked the farm they'd bought on the county line south of Wiarton, but by 1880 Albert and Bess had decided to move their growing brood into the village proper. Albert had been offered the post of customs officer to deal with traffic and goods coming in from American ports, and thought he might also open a general store, like the ones he'd run in the past. Within the year he had set up a shop that sold dry goods and clothing. He called himself the elephant. "When the elephant shakes his trunk," his newspaper ad promised, "he means business. . . ."

In a studio portrait of Albert taken around that time he looks very much like a town father. He's half-sitting, half-standing, jauntily straddling the corner of a table covered in a bear hide, his silk top hat upside down on the fur. His black moustache is curled and greased at the ends like a circus strongman's, his wavy hair is parted on the side and flattened with pomade. He's wearing a dark coat and grey pinstriped pants, one hand on his hip, the other clasping leather gloves. He looks like a nineteenth-century cartoon capitalist vaguely ill at ease in the pose, as if this was the photographer's idea of how a man of his stature should appear.

There's another photo that is more like the Albert Tyson his children and grandchildren described. The picture is torn and creased; it looks like it was carried for years in a pocket. He's older in this photograph, standing rather proudly in a studio with another man. Their clothes are wrinkled and Albert's beard looks rough and prickly. He's holding a fishing rod, while his friend carries a net. They both have leather straps attached to wicker fishing baskets across their chests and between them nine enormous, silvery trout flash in the photographer's light.

Albert remained an eager fisherman his whole life, and even bought an island in the archipelago known as the Fishing Islands, which runs along the Lake Huron side of the Bruce Peninsula from the village of Oliphant north to Pike Bay. Long a traditional fishing ground for the Saugeen Ojibway, the seventy-odd islands were known for the schools of herring, whitefish, sturgeon and trout that passed among their shoals and inlets. The fish were said to be so plentiful they lifted each other out of the water. One story has it that in the 1880s a Mohawk named Jack Martin sold the islands to the Crown for seventy-five cents apiece—without the permission of the Saugeen. Martin hightailed it out of his adopted reservation, money in hand, but his deal stuck and the Crown began offering the islands, crammed with cedar and poison ivy, for sale.

Albert Tyson was one of the early buyers. At first the family spent summers camped on a wooded island just off the shore near the village of Red Bay. Albert built a small sawmill and harvested the trees there. The logs would be rafted to the mainland where there was a makeshift railway with horse-drawn carts leading toward the village.

The family used to claim that the streets of Detroit were built using cedar logs cut in the area.

When the Tysons arrived at their cottage each summer they would come by horse and carriage. It was a trip of about two hours from Wiarton on the rough roads and they had to be prepared to do some walking when the wheels got stuck. Passing the wooden bridge and the low muddy road near Sky Lake they'd invariably be forced to dismount and walk up the hill toward the lake, each child charged with carrying a bag or basket. Then they'd leave the horses and carriages at a stable on the shore and row over to the island with their supplies. According to an oft-repeated family story, it was when Albert got lost rowing over to join his wife and children late one foggy Friday night that he decided once and for all to trade in the island for some property on the mainland.

The cottage Albert built on the shore just south of Golden Valley Bay had a view of their former island, still known as Tyson, and access to a long, wide, sandy beach. Looking out onto the water, the Tysons could watch skiffs and fishing schooners sailing by, as well as steamers bound for Goderich and Southampton. The larger boats gave the Fishing Islands a wide berth; the depths and shallows of the archipelago were said to contain the shattered hulls of many unfortunate vessels.

As the Tyson family grew, the cottage became their gathering spot, the glue holding the eight children and their parents together. Much later, when some of the boys had moved West, and the girls had married and left for other towns, they would all come home at least once in the summer to spend time at "the lake." There would be fishing expeditions and sailing races. The grandchildren would comb the beaches along the shore searching for fragments of shipwrecks: a shard of rock-washed glass from a lantern that once swung from a schooner's cabin, a coin or brass fitting. They'd dare one another to sneak at night into the nearby cemetery where drowned sailors were buried.

From the beginning Albert Tyson called their patch of shoreline Petrel Point. At first he thought the flocks of small, dark birds he saw circling overhead were stormy petrels. Though he was mistaken—the petrel is an oceanic bird—the designation stuck. And in fact, there is something eerily appropriate about such a name on this wind-blown, shipwreck-strewn shore. In maritime mythology, stormy petrels are said to represent the souls of dead sailors.

In a box of memorabilia that my grandmother Eleanor inherited from her mother, Lillie, there are many pictures of the Tyson family at Petrel Point. Happy, laughing children gathering wood, girls in cotton dresses meant as bathing costumes, sailboats heeling in a stiff breeze. Lillie is the eldest, but she is small, with striking, catlike eyes and a high wide forehead. She looks serious. Also in the box is an autograph album that belonged to her when she was a girl. It is the size of a small woman's hand and has an ornate, illustrated cloth cover featuring two children picking fruit. The outside is wrinkled and yellowed with age, but inside, the paper is creamy, the pages edged with gold.

Near the front is an inscription from the friend whose gift it was in June 1884: "Within this book so pure and white/Let none but friends presume to write./And each line with friendship given/Direct the reader's thoughts to heaven."

It was several years, however, before Lillie Tyson had a chance to use her tantalizingly empty album. Perhaps there wasn't anyone she wanted a signature from at home in Wiarton or in Berlin, Ontario, where she taught for two years. Who needs the autograph of people you see every day? But she brought the album with her when she left for teacher's training at the Toronto Normal School in 1887. Going to the Normal in the heart of the bustling, busy, electrified city was the most exciting thing that had ever happened to her. She wanted a record of it.

Everything was different in Toronto: the clang of the trolleys and the *clack clack clack* of horses' hooves and wagon wheels on cobblestone streets, grimy little boys riding bicycles at breakneck speed, ringing their shiny bells at anyone who got in their way. And you hardly knew you were on the water the city was so congested with buildings and people—a trip out to the suburbs of Parkdale or Balmy Beach was the only way to really feel the cool, reassuring wind off Lake Ontario.

The Normal was in the thick of it all on a six-acre lot north of the harbour. The once-swampy property had been carefully cultivated with manicured gardens and stately old trees—each a different specimen—from around the world. It was the first training institute for teachers in the province. The other young women and men in her class had, like her, graduated from high school and most had already taught at small rural schools. At the Normal, they continued their education with algebra, chemistry, bookkeeping, English and "the art of teaching." There was a model school on the grounds where they could practise their skills. Rules were strict, especially for the girls. Students liked to say they were worked to the bone.

While the class of '87 was waiting for spring-exam results, Lillie passed around her autograph album. Her friends and classmates filled the pages with signatures and silly ditties. "Yours truly, Charlie Simmons, Toronto, 1887; Yours in trouble, Maria Gilcurry, 1887"; "You ask me to write in your album/Shall I write of the Normal School/With its pleasant trees and garden/And very absurd old rule!/Alas! Any poetic spirit has departed. Yours sincerely, Annie Simpson. Elora, 1887." Several others, mindful of posterity, quoted Goethe.

When her marks came in, Lillie pressed a rose from the Normal's gardens into her autograph book and packed it among her things. It would be hard to leave Toronto and return to the quiet streets of Wiarton. The village didn't even have a telephone and the sidewalks were merely wooden planks slapped down over the mud. Lillie's new friends who lived in the city teased her about teaching at a "rooral skool." They laughed that she'd have to empty the children's pockets of flasks of whisky before she got down to teaching; that she'd have to haul water miles and miles just to wash the blackboards. She'd have muscles like a logger in no time.

But it wasn't modern conveniences twenty-year-old Lillie Tyson would miss most about Toronto. The stories I've been told about my great-grandmother portray her as a romantic, a Victorian aesthete. It was culture that she longed for when she moved back home. The chance to wander the hallways of the museum on the grounds of the Normal. There were paintings there and sculpture and artifacts that the school's founder had brought back from Europe. She would miss talking with the other students and teachers about ideas, about Mrs. Browning and Lord Byron.

All her life, Lillie loved to read and recite, to paint and play the organ. One of the most vivid memories my grandmother Eleanor had about her own childhood was reciting poems that her mother had instructed her to memorize. Eleanor never forgot the words, and had an impressive repertoire of Shakespeare and Browning that she would pull out to dazzle her daughters.

In the Ontario of 1887, however, there weren't many options for a literary-minded young girl from a frontier village. Lillie was expected to go back to Wiarton after finishing at the Normal. She had a job at an elementary school nearby. Her mother and father would never have allowed her to go to Toronto if they thought she wouldn't return. They considered some education good for a woman; too much would make her ugly. When Lillie graduated in December 1887, she packed up her clothes and books and headed home.

When Lillie Tyson married Jim Crawford she had to give up her
teaching post, but she didn't give up her ambition.

Chapter 4

THE TURKEY TRAIL

BY ALL APPEARANCES, Lillie Tyson and Jim Crawford were a suitable match. Though he was her senior by thirteen years and had been married once before, he was widely considered—by those who discussed such things—to be a desirable bachelor. He was ambitious, well liked and though rather small in stature, had winning good looks with his dark shiny hair and deep brown eyes. Widowers were expected to remarry after a suitable grieving period and his wife had been dead nearly two and a half years when he asked Lillie Tyson for her hand.

For her part, Lillie was mature in the way the eldest child of eight must be. She'd been a teacher, was well read and cultured by the standards of the little village. She was attractive, too, if you could bear the intensity of her gaze and those startling eyes.

Albert, Lillie's father, approved of the marriage. The Crawfords were a promising lot. Everyone knew Jack through his myriad business ventures, and Middleton, of course, had made the village proud with his inventions. The family hadn't always been Temperance types like the Tysons, but after his marriage to Jennie Finch—who was the devoted recording scribe and officer of the Wiarton Division of the Sons of Temperance—Jim Crawford had sworn off liquor. He had also become part of the congregation at the Disciples—the first brick church in the village—where the Tysons had worshipped since arriving in Wiarton. Albert made no secret of the fact that he hoped Jim and Lillie would produce grandchildren for him soon.

It was December 3, 1889, when Lilias Elizabeth Tyson and James Victor Crawford took their vows before family and friends in the parlour of her parents' home. The Reverend Mr. Brown stood beneath a horseshoe of pine boughs in the front window, the play of mottled light through the crystallized ice on the windowpanes like a kaleidoscope on the floor around them. Lillie wore a brown silk crepe dress with a delicate ruffle around the hem and at her throat. She carried trailing English ivy in one hand, the square of handmade lace her aunt Jane had given her that morning clutched tightly in the other.

Jim and Lillie had decided to have the wedding once the *Agnes* was in dry dock so that they would have a chance to get away on a honeymoon. They planned to travel by train around southern Ontario and get to know one another better.

Lillie had to give up her teaching post when she married, but she didn't give up her intellectual ambition. For many years she hosted literary teas and read every novel and newspaper she could get her hands on.

My grandmother inherited many of her books. Some of them were passed on to my mother, and my parents now have a small, decaying library of Lillie's Byron and Sir Walter Scott, the leather-bound collected works of Shakespeare and Elizabeth Barrett Browning. The most extraordinary thing about the books, however, is not the glimmer of insight they offer into Lillie's intellectual preoccupations, but the objects she tucked inside. Christmas notes and photographs, flattened grocery bills and dried flowers waft out when I open them. An inveterate clipper of newspapers and magazines, Lillie pressed poems and articles into each volume, staining the pages with brown shadows.

The books are like treasure chests. Each time I visit my parents I take them down from the shelf and invariably discover some tiny photo or crumbling maple leaf I haven't seen before. And even if there is no new morsel, there are always important passages Lillie underlined two or three times. "Trust thyself," advises Ralph Waldo Emerson from her edition of *The Works of Emerson*. I can almost hear Lillie nodding in agreement and whispering, "A foolish consistency is the hobgoblin of little minds" as she drew her pencil beneath the words.

With dreams embroidered by poetry and art, her sense of a larger world fostered by education and time spent away, Lillie was restless. In photographs she exudes an unmistakable determination, even fierceness. It is striking, then, that so many of the notations and clippings in her books emphasize the Christian ideal of accepting one's circumstances with grace and humility. It's almost as if she needed to convince herself.

          ⟡

May 22, 1891, Wiarton village

The baby is fussing. He's just eaten and had his nappy changed. Lillie wishes sometimes he could just tell her what's wrong. Even though she looked after her brothers and sisters when they were little, having her own child is different. She doesn't remember them being so demanding. So insistent. Every cry like an arrow in her belly.

Her mother and sisters have been helpful these past few months, visiting and cooking meals, but Lillie is still finding it difficult. She's always alone these days with Jim on the water.

She knew what she was getting into when she married a lake captain. She knew she'd be alone most of the shipping season. He stops in for a day each week, sometimes less, then he's off again up the coast, to Manitoulin Island or the northeastern shore and the lakehead—the Turkey Trail people call it, because the route resembles nothing so much as the bird's erratic meanderings. And she knew that there would be moments when she'd be frightened for him and herself and their little family. Like last autumn when she was expecting for the first time and he was out on the *Agnes* when snow started blowing. In a blink, Colpoy's Bay became a snarl of white waves, spray flying nearly as high as the cliffs. Lillie had lived on Georgian Bay long enough to know that it was worse out in the open.

Still, she didn't anticipate being *lonely*. Not with her brothers and sisters, her painting and her books. But it's different now that she and Jim have their own family. She doesn't have time for poetry and reading. It's mothering all the time.

There are some master's wives who go with their husbands on the boats. Captain Angus Macaulay, whose nephew is Jim's friend John Macaulay, has his wife in the galley of the *Jones*. But many of the sailors think it's unlucky to have women on board. Anyway, Lillie isn't one for the water. She travelled on the steamers as a girl, taking day trips for picnics or the fresh air. But she doesn't relish the prospect of being in close quarters with the kind of men who work on her husband's tugs, their tattoos and rude language, the drinking and bravado. And the lake seems entirely unpredictable to her. Jim says it isn't, that if you know the depths and landmarks, if you can read the glass and rely on your men, if you've been along the coast and through the open of Georgian Bay as many times as he has, it is sure as sunrise every time.

Lillie rocks little Albert Victor in her arms as he makes grunting noises. Her father was touched when she named the baby for him. He adores the child. People keep saying what an easy baby he is. And he is sweet when others are around. But when it's just the two of them, the child gets cranky, as if he is bored with his own mother. He cries all the time.

Lillie tut-tuts, but Albert starts wailing anyway. She carries him to the window where they can see out to the harbour.

The arrival of Jim's new boat, named *A. V. Crawford* for little Albert, is important news in the village. Her mother and father are coming over soon to pick her up so she and the baby can be there when Jim arrives. A new dock was even built to accommodate the tug. Jim was over in Goderich several times this winter checking on the progress at Marlton's boatyard. Lillie heard Jim tell her father that this new steamer will be even faster than the *Jones*.

Swaying back and forth to keep Albert quiet, Lillie reaches up to tuck back an errant strand of hair from her forehead. She did it up in a new way this morning. For the occasion. People will be watching her, the young captain's wife. She wants to look her best.

At least the men who work in the harbour respect her husband. His crew treat him with deference. When Lillie goes out for a walk, even without Jim, all the sailors take off their hats, even stepping off the sidewalk into the mud when she passes. And he does well for himself, makes a decent living. It's not all bad, being married to a sailor.

Lillie especially loves their red-brick house, with its scalloped gingerbread and circle cut-outs framing the peaks of the roof and two porches. She and her mother planted a large south-facing garden last year. There are other grander homes nearby but theirs has a view of the harbour and a fine location on the hill leading out of town. Last summer before she knew she was expecting, Lillie hung baskets of lobelia and purple verbena from the arched portico over the side porch. She would sit out in the morning with a cup of tea and a book. She'll do the same this year if she has a spare moment to think about something other than little Master Albert Victor Crawford.

❦

March 9, 1893, a drive in the country

Lillie's younger brother Will is coming over to take her for a drive in the democrat. She has barely left the house these past months with Albert just two, and a second baby on the way. Jim's been so busy. He and Jack have just bought another new steamer and they've been holed up with it for weeks in the company's sheds. People say it's going to be an early opening of navigation. Jim comes home every night smelling of the mixture of lye and soap they use to clean the whitework. It rubs his fingers so raw they split and bleed.

Will has insisted on taking Lillie out, saying it will be good for her to see the buds on the trees, to get out for a ride while she still can. He needs some air himself after studying all winter for his sailing master's papers. Mother has agreed to look after Albert while they're gone.

It's a fine day for a drive. There's a chill in the air, but it's fresh in that expectant way of the first nice day after a long winter. Split-rail fences line the dirt road leading south. They wave to friends and acquaintances. "Beautiful day!" someone shouts. Will whistles happily under his breath.

But on the edge of the village, up the hill near McLarens,' Lillie feels tingling in her arms and legs. She can't focus. Then, suddenly, before she has a chance to say anything to Will, everything is black. Her entire body goes limp.

Her brother doesn't notice at first, so possessed is he by the smells of spring, by being young and strong, his life laid out before him like a book. But when Lillie sinks down in her seat, he pulls the carriage to an abrupt stop.

"Are you all right?" he says, shaking his sister gently by the shoulders. Panic makes his voice rise. When she doesn't respond, Will lifts her up and off the democrat. Her pregnancy makes her unwieldy and he struggles, embarrassed by her floppy, heavy body. When he gets her onto the ground he lays her down carefully on his jacket and shakes her again.

"Lillie! Lillie, can you hear me?"

When she still doesn't answer, Will runs to the nearby house for help. One of the McLaren children is dispatched bareback on the farm horse to fetch the doctor in town while Will rushes back to Lillie's side. Mrs. McLaren follows with blankets and smelling salts to pass beneath Lillie's nose; Will applies cool cloths to her forehead. Neither of them speak.

By the time the doctor arrives half an hour later, Lillie is conscious but disoriented, and she can't move the left side of her body. Will and the McLarens were too afraid to move her before but now the men gingerly lift her inside. After a brief examination, the doctor says it must have been a stroke of paralysis. Youth and good health, he says, are in her favour but such attacks can be fatal. The baby might have suffered, he whispers to Will in the back kitchen.

No one expects Lillie to live. It's the kind of sudden and mysterious illness that has killed people much stronger than Lillie Tyson Crawford. The congregation at the Disciples includes a special prayer for her in the Sunday service. People gather at the house to pat Jim's hand and pray for her recovery.

Over the next two weeks Lillie slowly regains her strength. Her left arm remains limp at her side, and occasionally when she stands her left leg gives out and she collapses like a wooden marionette whose strings have been dropped. Sometimes, out of nowhere, uncontrollable sobs wrack her body with their violence. But it's clear Lillie isn't going to die.

On All Fools' Day, 1893, a month after her stroke, Lillie gives birth to a baby boy. He is small but healthy. They call him James Tyson Crawford. The family worries over him.

Lillie remains in bed for several months after the birth. Her mother and sisters care for her, the house and the two children. By September she can walk again, but she is frail and has lost a great deal of weight. Her left arm still hangs uselessly. When she's sitting she tucks it into her lap, as if it were someone else's limb she's temporarily caring for.

Her mother, Bess, suggests gently that they consider finding a nursemaid for the children, and Lillie bursts into tears. But she needs the help. Jim is away so much. She worries about him now more than ever. Whenever he's out on the water she watches the bay from their front window, scrutinizing the waves and the force of the wind, praying for herself and her babies and for him.

In Wiarton people treated passage on Georgian Bay casually,
and grew used to tasting the wind for the flavour of a storm,
to putting their trust in the Old Man.

Chapter 5

THE SHIPPING NEWS

THE STAKES WERE HIGH for Jim Crawford and the other captains of Georgian Bay steamboats. They were constantly forced to gamble with the weather, because whatever boat arrived first at the small, northern ports would win the day's business. It became a kind of game. In the 1880s and 1890s, the shipping news in all the little hometown papers around the bay were filled with tales of speed trials, of honour won and lost, of small tugs taking on bigger, stronger, faster steamers, captains risking everything to be first into port.

There were some masters who became legendary. Black Pete Campbell was one. A fierce competitor based out of Collingwood, the daredevil Scot with twinkling dark eyes was notorious for heading out in a storm, setting course and then leaving the ship in the hands of his crew while he settled confidently into his bunk for a catnap. It wasn't his temperament that earned Black Pete the nickname, but his jet-black hair and the way he sculpted his beard and shaved off his moustache so that his face appeared pink and bare, framed by bushy sideburns that melted into thick whiskers on his chin and cheeks.

Sailors all over the lake talked about how Campbell would take on any captain who showed a hint of interest in racing. Lurking near the mouth of Owen Sound at the helm of the *Pacific*, Black Pete would challenge Monsieur F. X. LaFrance, the daring French-Canadian master of the sidewheeler *Carmona*, to a speed trial. "First to Killarney," he'd shout, and off they'd go, past Presqu'ile, and the islands at the mouth of Colpoy's Bay, belching clouds of black smoke, burning the paint off their stacks from the heat.

It was exhilarating. Dangerous. The wooden boats sometimes hit rocks and sank like stones, dragging people and freight with them, and they regularly caught fire, burning to soggy, charred embers. Yet for his first twenty-five years on the bay, Black Pete didn't have a single major mishap. When he stopped in Wiarton one day the *Echo* described him as "so well and favourably known on the upper lakes that the travelling public will always feel a sense of safety while on his boat." It's thanks to this sterling reputation that the day his luck ran out only added to the lustre of his image.

It was the ill-fated spring of 1882, Jim Crawford's first year on the water; Black Pete was at the helm of the steamer *Manitoulin*, heading down Manitowaning Bay with a full load of passengers and cargo destined for Manitoulin Island and the northeastern shore. The captain was just sitting down to lunch in the ship's gracious dining room when suddenly, from deep inside the wooden boat, someone cried, "Fire!"

When Black Pete arrived breathless in the engine room, it was in flames, the junior engineers already forced from their posts by choking smoke and a fire so hot it sent slivers of blue heat shooting into the air. Leaving the chief engineer to hold the throttle open at top speed, Black Pete rushed back to the dining room, shouting at the passengers to put on their life preservers and prepare for anything.

Lifeboats were swung out and at the ready, but people were terrified, threatening to jump. Warning them to sit tight and await his instructions, Black Pete made his way to the pilothouse where he ordered a change of course, and headed the ship, full steam ahead, toward the shore about a mile away.

The fire was raging out of control, feeding on a fresh coat of spring paint, when someone remembered that five hundred pounds of blasting powder, a shipment for the Canadian Pacific Railway, was loaded on the storage deck. Deckhands rushed to push it off the boat before it exploded.

It took six minutes for the *Manitoulin* to hit the beach, the roof of the pilothouse on fire. The chief engineer, feeling the keel of the steamer grinding into the rocks and sand, escaped the inferno of the boiler room, jumping with the others into water so shallow they could wade to shore. But eleven passengers had panicked and jumped into the icy water minutes before the boat hit ground. They floundered helplessly, slowly giving in to the numbing water while the rest of the passengers and crew walked to safety. The captain was the last to leave the flaming boat. It's part of Black Pete's legend that when he finally jumped down onto the shore and ran away from the carcass of his ship, he had a small child tucked safely under his arm.

Within two days, everyone in the towns and villages around the perimeter of Georgian Bay had heard the news about Black Pete and the *Manitoulin*. But if the story made them worried about travelling by steamer on the inland sea, there was little they could do about it. The bay was a giant transit system—however rolling, rumbly and dangerous—and for many isolated people it was the only way to connect with the outside world.

Georgian Bay settlers accepted the dangers: the shoal-infested waters, fickle winds and raging weather, water-spouts, storm tides and hurricanes. They treated passage on the bay casually, and grew accustomed to tasting the wind for the flavour of a storm, to crossing their fingers and knocking on wood, to putting their trust in the Old Man, as everyone called the master of a steamboat.

The captains trusted, too, and navigated, they said, "By ear, by nose and by God." In moments of weakness or conceit, sailors sometimes claimed they knew the waters and winds so well they could navigate blindfolded. Which wasn't so far from reality: their tools of navigation were rudimentary, and large parts of the bay had never even been charted.

Henry Wolsey Bayfield of the British navy had surveyed what he could of Georgian Bay in the 1820s, taking two years to complete the painstaking work. Using a compass and sextant, plus a chronometer to measure differences in latitude, he charted the main channels and islands. A stickler for detail, Captain Bayfield had possessed a stiff-upper-lip sense of duty. Nothing the Royal Navy did—not the half pay he received or the miserably low wages of his crew—could rid the surveyor of the conviction that his work was for the greater good of Brittannia. He'd seen the fire in the eyes of the Yankees when he served during the War of 1812. He knew they would stop at nothing to get their greedy, republican hands on the lakes and riches of the Canadas. The survey, he never hesitated to remind his crew, would ensure Britain's continued dominion over the northern territories. From two six-oared boats, he and his cold, often mutinous men created detailed charts of the major ports, passages and islands. Bayfield would finish the drawings and descriptions at their winter post in Quebec. Between 1820 and 1822, he diligently catalogued and named the inlets, points and shoals, honouring royalty and fellow naval officers with large islands and sounds, giving the nod to family members and friends when the dignitaries ran out. It was he who named the whole body of water for his sovereign King George IV. The son of mad King George III, he was a good choice as a namesake. Over the years he revealed himself to be nearly as tempestuous and changeable as the bay.

But even though Captain Bayfield and his men were careful and exacting, they had no more than a lead line and sounding machine to take depth measurements; and they didn't venture into the thirty thousand islands along the northeast shore at all. That entire side of the bay, from somewhere north of Honey Harbour all the way up to Killarney, appears on Bayfield's chart as ill-defined pebbles and dotted lines. Plotting the tiny islands, narrow channels and hidden shoals would have consumed the rest of his career.

It took the devastating wreck of another passenger steamer, only four months after the *Manitoulin* went down, to provoke the Canadian government to revisit Captain Bayfield's charts.

The storm that sank the *Asia* came from the southwest, sweeping across Lake Huron, streaming through the Bruce Peninsula, doubling over pine trees, gathering force as it whipped the open water of Georgian Bay into furious waves. Many of the passengers on the 136-foot steamboat had been up all night the evening before, seasick, tossing in their berths or cots or their chairs on the deck, rolling with the top-heavy ship as it groaned and shook, exhausted from the strain of the wind and waves.

Duncan Tinkiss, an eighteen-year-old headed up to Manitoulin Island to work at his family's hotel in Manitowaning, didn't have any trouble sleeping. He'd shared a stateroom with his uncle and had hardly noticed the steamer's contortions. It was after breakfast, he told an inquest hastily pulled together in the lobby of a Parry Sound hotel after the wreck, that things started looking bad to him.

Built for canal work, the *Asia* had a narrow, shallow hull and a high cabin and upper works. In September 1882, she was temporarily employed as a replacement for the lost *Manitoulin* on the Great Northern Transit Company's

Collingwood to Sault Ste. Marie route. Hers was a rambling path along the eastern edge of the Bruce Peninsula, up to Manitoulin Island, then across northern Georgian Bay to the French River. After dropping off loggers and their supplies, she was scheduled to sail to Sault Ste. Marie. The trip would take several days. The boat wasn't built to withstand the full force of a Georgian Bay storm, but the *Asia*, with a heavy cargo in her hold, could stand up well. Unladen or unbalanced, however, she would give her captain trouble.

That early fall day in 1882, with the crisp bite of winter already in the air, the *Asia* was carrying a hundred passengers plus more than twenty crew, and was heavily loaded with supplies and animals bound for the lumber camps up north. Much of the freight was assembled on the main deck toward the back, with some extra cargo stowed up on the hurricane deck, the highest point on the boat.

Around 9 a.m. on September 14, with her bow riding high in the growing waves and the wind tossing her around, the crew of the *Asia* decided to cut loose a small sailboat that had been tied behind and was forcing the steamer off course. Under orders from Captain John Savage, the men also threw some freight overboard to try to balance the vessel. About an hour later, with the wind picking up and waves starting to overwhelm the main deck, the cows and horses tied at the bow of the boat, all wild eyes and bulging veins, were pitched into the churning bay.

Trapped in a deep depression between giant waves, the boat rolled madly. When his uncle shouted, "The boat is doomed!" Duncan Tinkiss grabbed his coat and hat and slipped a life preserver over his head. At the inquest, he recalled heading for the port side as the boat

listed starboard and then, with many of the other passengers, clambering up to the hurricane deck. But the
force of the waves must have already sliced the upper
works from the main cabin, because looking down Tinkiss
saw that it was only about four feet to the spitting,
sucking water below.

Christy Ann Morrison, the only other survivor of the
Asia, also testified at the inquest. A native of Owen Sound,
the teenager was headed to Sault Ste. Marie and from
there to Michigan to visit an aunt. She spent her first night
on the steamboat sick to her stomach and wide awake,
pitched back and forth in her berth. The next morning she
and most of the other passengers avoided breakfast, opting
instead to catch some more sleep in their staterooms or
wherever they could find it.

As far as Morrison could tell, the deciding moments
of the disaster came suddenly. Although she heard the
teeth-rattling screeches of the animals as they were shoved
overboard and saw other passengers desperately searching
for life preservers, her cousin, John MacDonald, the *Asia's*
first mate, reassured her that the captain and crew would
get the boat under control. She donned a life preserver
anyway and waited dutifully at the door of her cabin for
instructions. When the boat rolled on its side and water
started pouring into her cabin, she didn't wait any longer.
Rushing out to the deck on the upper side of the boat, she
grabbed frantically for the railing, and gripping it, slid
down the metal into the water. She sank for what seemed
forever, the pull of the sinking ship dragging her deeper
and deeper into the blackness. A dreamy haze slowed her
movements, the shock of submersion stopping time, but
then, suddenly, she was up, out of the water, gasping for air,

for solidity, her hands reaching for the side of a lifeboat. Her cousin, the first mate, helped drag her in.

Tinkiss found his way to the same boat, but only after abandoning another overloaded vessel that had flipped. To get away, he had to fight off fellow passengers who clawed at his life preserver, trying to tear it off his body. At the inquest he told investigators that he saw at least sixty people in the water or in lifeboats, all of them screaming and crying, begging for help, for safety, for respite from the waves and wind.

When Tinkiss climbed in the boat there were already about eighteen people in it. He noticed two other lifeboats similarly loaded with terrified passengers and crew. But the one he and Morrison found themselves in was the captain's own yawl and it was sturdier than the others. With a metal hull and flotation chambers under the seats, the vessel righted itself each time it was flipped over by the high waves. Morrison and Tinkiss watched through the spray as the other lifeboats turtled again and again, fewer survivors struggling to right them each time.

By the time darkness descended, the captain's lifeboat had capsized so many times only six men (including the captain, the first mate and Tinkiss) plus Christy Ann Morrison had survived. She and Tinkiss had endured by clinging to ropes tied off the bow and stern of the vessel, staying with the boat but avoiding the heavy slap of the hull as it flipped over. She didn't know how the others had managed. With a breeze from the west, the lifeboat drifted far from the scene of the disaster and its twisted wreckage.

By midnight, the survivors were freezing cold and exhausted, lacking the strength even to row. As the storm petered out and they drifted, Morrison's cousin tried to keep the others' spirits up by singing, "Pull for the shore, sailors, pull for the shore." The men joined in but they were weak and tired, struggling against the powerful urge to let go, to close their eyes and just fall asleep. When someone spotted the light at Byng Inlet there was a momentary burst of elation, but when an offshore breeze began to push them back toward the open, the men started to nod off. They never woke up.

Morrison's story of her cousin's final moments gripped the readers of newspapers and tabloids across the country. He "put his head up to my face in the dark and asked if it was me. I said 'Yes.' My hair was flying around, and he seized it in his death grip and pulled down my head. I asked the captain, who was near, to release my hair. He did so, and the mate soon breathed his last."

The captain, deliriously issuing orders to imaginary crewmen, his head in Duncan Tinkiss's lap, died soon afterward. The teenagers sat at opposite ends of the lifeboat, the bodies of the others filling the gap between them like unspoken words. They drifted that way all night, each nodding off despite promises to the other that they would stay awake. But as the morning sun opened like an eye across the eastern horizon, they both woke to find smooth rocks and gnarled trees before them. It was the island maze of Pointe au Baril. They had drifted more than forty miles from their wrecked ship.

When the teenagers finally made it to shore, Tinkiss removed the bodies of the dead men from their lifeboat. Morrison watched him work from a spot on the cool rock. She was exhausted, rooted there, as if her last remaining particles of energy were being absorbed by the granite. She thought she might never be able to stand again. But when the grisly work of removing the bodies was finished, the two set off in their boat for what they thought was a lighthouse in the distance. It took the rest of the day to paddle to a nearby island with oars they had picked up. The next morning they set off again, but soon discovered that what they had hoped was a lighthouse was merely an empty derrick. Bitterly disappointed, they resigned themselves to dying of exposure in the chill September air.

That evening, an Ojibway couple out picking blackberries found the teenagers hungry and frightened but very much alive, curled up on cedar branches, nightmares animating their sleeping faces. For the price of Tinkiss's gold watch, the couple took the two survivors on the daylong sail to the town of Parry Sound.

A photograph of Christy Ann Morrison, taken in a studio after the wreck, was made into a collector's card. On the back there's a brief summary of the events and an explanation of the photo: "The Portrait on the reverse side is that of Christy Ann Morrison, the only lady survivor [of the *Asia*]...." Indeed, she's dressed like a lady in a corset and a long, fringed and intricately trimmed black dress. The painting of a coastal scene on the backdrop was somebody's idea of an appropriately nautical set and she's holding a rough ship's rope that leads out of the picture. Her eyes are downcast and slightly mournful. But it's her hair that you notice first. Calculated to appear disheveled, it is tangled and wavy, a black curtain to her waist. She is a reluctant Lady of the Lake.

In the days following the *Asia* disaster, the national newspapers did a brisk trade in sermons about the nature of the coffin ships plying Georgian Bay. Captain Savage was blamed for his lack of judgment. The company was blamed for its greed. The government was blamed for failing to regulate the industry properly. At least one story that leaked into the press seemed to justify the hectoring. A Toronto butcher named Joseph Shipp had been aboard the boat on the Collingwood to Owen Sound portion of the voyage. But he had become worried about the number of passengers and amount of freight on the high, narrow ship. He didn't like the look of the horses tied at the bow, or the deck covered in crates of cast-iron pots and pressed hay, or the way the steamer rolled recklessly in the waves. His fears were confirmed when he overheard a conversation between the captain and the boat inspector in Owen Sound harbour. "I know this about her," Shipp recalled the inspector saying loudly. "She won't go out of here tonight. If she does, she won't reach French River. . . . She's strained." Shipp watched incredulously as the captain brushed off the inspector's concerns and walked away. When he saw four more heavy milk cows led up the gangway into the *Asia*'s hold, Shipp grabbed his bags and bolted.

With more than 120 people drowned, the wreck of the *Asia* affected every town and village on the bay. People pored over the tragic stories that drifted in. Two members of the well-known Sparks family of Ottawa, the publisher of the Parry Sound *North Star* and the son of Collingwood boat builder William Watts were all lost. Trunks and chairs and children's books were discovered. Pillow slips were found floating like heavy cream on the surface of the water, the word *Asia* stitched along the hem.

The wreck of the steamboat and the teenagers' story of survival against the odds became a long-playing drama in the daily papers. The public began to demand that something be done to make Georgian Bay and the steamers plying its waters safer for passengers and trade.

Prime Minister Sir John A. Macdonald, recently re-elected for the third time, acted with his characteristic talent for political manoeuvre. Within a year of the *Asia's* foundering, the government had begun a new hydrographical survey of the bay and Lake Huron. The inquest into the wreck had uncovered no evidence that the steamer sank because of navigational difficulties or an unmarked shoal, but a new chart of the region would do much to calm the country's collective nerves.

In August 1883, Staff Commander John George Boulton was entrusted with the task of charting Georgian Bay. Another meticulous and principled man, he would spend most of the next ten years working from an old 110-foot steamer renamed the *Bayfield*. The maps that Captain Boulton and his men produced were so accurate some of them are still in use today.

But the reality was, the wreck of the *Asia* probably rattled politicians in Ottawa more than it did the sailors of Georgian Bay. Undoubtedly they were shaken by the loss of friends, relatives and colleagues, but many of the men on the docks felt the boat was doomed from the beginning. It wasn't made for sailing on the open water. The company had been criticized for years for sending overloaded boats out onto the lake; and sailors reminded one another that the company was also known for hiring men who couldn't get a job with more respectable shipping lines. Even the new charts meant little to the old masters, who said they'd been drawn up by people who'd never lived on the lake. In order to get them into circulation, the government was forced to give them away. Sailors complained that the new surveyors didn't venture beyond the coast's main channels into the small bays and inlets where the small steamboats operated.

Of course, a lack of charts had never stopped experienced masters before. Settlers and loggers and fishermen still needed supplies, log booms had to be tugged to the sawmills and the catch brought down from the remote fishing grounds. The sailors shared information about shallow water and favoured passages, passing news from boat to boat.

The Crawford quickly proved a welcome addition to the fleet.
Her launch gave the Crawford brothers and the town
a much-needed boost.

Chapter 6

THE WILDCAT WHISTLE

BY THE BEGINNING of the 1890s, Jim Crawford had established himself as an integral part of the sailing community in Wiarton. He was widely acknowledged to be one of the best navigators in the area, and the Crawford brothers' shipping business was a homegrown success story. They decided to incorporate, calling themselves the Crawford Tug Company, Ltd. Jim took the title of president and Jack was the secretary. They chose a woodcut of a small tugboat to appear on all official correspondence.

The boat is a sturdy-looking little craft with lots of deck space for freight, an upright wooden cabin and wheel-house, flags flying at both bow and stern. A cloud of smoke trails from her funnel, a symbol of the company's speed and efficiency.

Jack Crawford had also become active in other business ventures. In 1890 he and several others brought limited electricity to Wiarton when they bought an old steam-powered electric plant. A year later, he purchased the long-abandoned gristmill.

Jack also took care of his brother Middleton's investments in Canada. After the patent for his gold-refining process made him a wealthy man, Middleton had become a small-time mining magnate, using the "Crawford method" at mines he co-owned near Belleville, Ontario, and in Cripple Creek, Colorado. Jack would often join him when he went abroad, visiting his business interests.

Jim Crawford wasn't like his cosmopolitan brothers. While they travelled the world, scouting for mining properties in Mexico and the U.S., cruising to France and England on luxury ships, he stayed at home. He visited the gold mine near Belleville once. But the farthest he usually ventured was to Toronto for the annual September Industrial Fair. Jim liked Wiarton with its familiar streets and harbour: the whistle of the schooners' halyards, the howl of the wind as it swung down the bay, stirring the water into stern little white caps. Georgian Bay offered its own kinds of challenges.

Besides, he was busy. Wiarton was growing. In 1894, it incorporated, declaring itself a town. His family was also expanding. Despite Lillie's continued ill health, she gave birth to two more children before the century was over.

And Jim had become active in the Young Men's Liberal-Conservative Club, as well as the board of trade and Cedar Lodge Masons.

The shipping business was also changing. While there was still lots of demand for towing and hauling, doing salvage work and carrying cargo, by 1890 word had filtered south about the cleansing and rejuvenating properties of Georgian Bay, the delicate flavours of the fish, the rugged beauty of the landscape. Steamboat tourism was becoming big business.

The large luxury ships owned by the Canadian Pacific Railway stuck to the deep waters and marked channels, travelling from Owen Sound and Collingwood through the open bay to the locks at Sault Ste. Marie and the head of Lake Superior. They were 300-foot, steel vessels that boasted lavish first-class cabins. The wealthy tourists expected white-linen dining, spacious staterooms and nightly entertainment. Second-class compartments were crammed with workers and immigrants headed to what promoters liked to call the Wild and Woolly West.

But the small local steamers were also in demand, offering berths to passengers interested in visiting the shallow harbours of villages along the shores of the bay. Intrepid American tourists and loggers headed to timber limits in the north, businessmen plying their trade in isolated regions, as well as clergymen, fishermen and farmers took the coasting boats. Often, these steamers would do double duty, taking people and supplies upbound, then loading the hold with fish packed in ice to be carried southward.

In Wiarton, the Buffalo Fish Company's steamer *Jones* took care of much of the local passenger trade. She had always had a few berths available to travellers, but in 1891 the steamer was fitted out and licensed to accommodate twenty paying passengers.

The *Jones* had few of the luxuries of the big CPR vessels, but there were still sightseeing opportunities and card-playing, a chance to shoot seagulls from the deck. Captain Angus Macaulay commanded the steamer for most of the 1890s, and was known to be especially accommodating to passengers, offering salty anecdotes about the passing scenery and water traffic. He liked to show off the *Jones*'s engines, pushing her to her top speed of eighteen miles an hour.

Each week, the boat would stop in at fishing stations off the south coast of Manitoulin Island and along the northeast shore—Killarney, the Bustards, Byng Inlet and Pointe au Baril—dropping off passengers and picking up as much as ten tons of fish a season from a single camp. The *Jones* would announce her arrival with a shriek of her famous steam whistle. People said it sounded like a screeching wildcat: a treble WHEE-E-E that would rattle your teeth, then a lower bass O-O-O and back to a treble that echoed off the rocks in the small harbours.

The outpost fishermen looked forward to the *Jones* making port, pulling up nets and hurrying back to camp when they heard her unmistakable whistle. Sometimes the *Jones* would be carrying letters and newspapers, maybe tobacco and whisky. Several times a season there would be a representative from the Buffalo Fish Company on board, sent north with a bag full of cash to pay the fishermen for their labours.

People in Wiarton also looked forward to seeing the *Jones*. The crew were all local men. Townspeople often travelled on her. They considered the *Jones* their boat. So when news of a collision with Black Pete's old steamer, the *Pacific*, reached Wiarton, it caused something of a sensation.

It was September 1898, almost midnight. The *Jones* was three miles from Kagawong Harbour on Manitoulin Island and the watch had just changed. The wheelsman was down below when Captain Macaulay saw the lights of the much-larger *Pacific* bearing down on them from the opposite direction.

Darkness on the water is hard to measure. One's eyes can adjust to it over time, seeking out gradients of blue-black to indicate land, tree or rock. The moon can light up the water like a searchlight, but without that guidance, without lights on shore or the glow of electricity in the distance, it is as if there is no far, only near.

That September night, Captain Macaulay could see the running lights of the oncoming boat but couldn't immediately gauge the distance between his steamer and the *Pacific*. He heard her captain give two short blasts of her steam whistle, an indication that she would take the port side. He acknowledged with his own whistle. But a few moments later he realized that the *Jones* would hit shore if he held his course. He signalled his alarm; he would need to take the other side. But by then the boats were almost upon each other. Captain Macaulay gave the bells to stop and back up but it was too late. The vessels collided, the iron-plated bow of the *Pacific* ramming the *Jones*'s port side. The *Jones* shuddered and then cracked, splinters from an enormous gouge near the bow shooting along the steamer's hull.

The *Jones* began to sink almost immediately, taking on water through the gash. The *Pacific* had escaped relatively unscathed, so the *Jones*'s crew and passengers quickly jumped to safety on her deck. But they soon realized that one of their company was missing.

The stern of the steamer was sinking, disappearing into the dark, bubbling water when Captain Macaulay ordered two crew members back on board to search for the passenger, an old woman from Tobermory. They calculated that the front section of the *Jones* would be held afloat for a few minutes by the empty fish boxes in the bow, and the two men jumped onto the boat, forcing their way into the woman's small stateroom. They found the seventy-year-old grandmother snoring loudly, unperturbed by the rapidly sinking vessel. The men carried her, still in her nightclothes, out to the waiting boat. They watched from the deck of the *Pacific* as nine minutes after the collision, the *Jones* disappeared into the smoky water.

The wooden steamboats of the late nineteenth century sank with alarming regularity. If they were salvageable they were simply repaired and put back to work. The *Jones* was no exception. The steamer, resting in only forty feet of water, was raised a month after she sank. By mid-December 1898, she was fully repaired and ready for service.

For two more seasons, the Buffalo Fish Company kept the *J. H. Jones* on her regular route. But changes in the company's ownership (after 1899 it was known as Dominion Fish Company), as well as the expected launch of several new vessels, prompted them to offer the *Jones* for sale.

In the fall of 1900, the Crawford Tug Company gladly put down cash for the *Jones*. They planned to expand their passenger business from one steamer, the *Joe Milton* (which they'd bought when they traded in the *A. V. Crawford* in 1895), to two.

For the first few seasons, the *Jones* actually remained on her old Dominion Fish route, taking supplies and passengers up to the company's fishing stations and bringing the catch home to the processing plant in Wiarton. Later, once Dominion had launched its new steamers, Crawford Tug put the *Jones* on a twice-a-week round trip up to Manitoulin Island and the North Shore, stopping in at Killarney, the Bustards and Pointe au Baril. They advertised the trip in the *Echo:* "The Crawford Tug Co. Str. Jones, J.V. Crawford, Master, Leaves WIARTON every MONDAY evening and FRIDAY at 10 A.M. . . . Fare for the round trip only $7, including meals and berth, to see these picturesque islands and fishing stations."

On weekends and evenings or when business was slow, the steamer was hired out as an excursion boat. In the summer, Sunday-school groups and Orange Lodge revellers would rent the *Jones* and her crew for trips up the coast. Years later, people would recall that on nights when the moon was full Old Man Crawford would take the local high school kids out for a cruise, the sky on the water shimmering silver and light. He'd charge them a total of $5.00 for a trip to the mouth of the bay and back. The young people would collect twenty-five cents from each passenger to pay him, with any extra money raised going to the school. On the way back, they'd beg Captain Crawford to move in close at Spirit Rock, where water stains and deep cuts in the limestone trace the outline of a girl's face. Leaning in close, someone would claim she'd heard ghostly whispers, the teary lament of the Spirit Maiden who threw herself from the cliff when she and her lover were spurned by her tribe. Calling out as they passed the rock etched with her face, the young people believed the echoes there were louder than anywhere on the entire shore.

These cruises made Jim Crawford a sentimental favourite among local people. After his death, the newspapers invariably referred to him as one of the bay's most popular captains. He was said to possess superior navigating skills and to be especially commendable for never having had a serious accident—despite the fact that he was known to go out when others chose to stay in port. But while it was true that he'd never lost a steamer on his watch, he had, in fact, lost crew. It was the events of May 1900 that people would remember most of all.

On the *Joe Milton*'s first trip of the season, Jim was in the wheelhouse and the boat was steaming along off the southern coast of Manitoulin, tentacles of spring wind riffling though the deckhands' sweaters and caps. The steamer was about eleven miles off the harbour at Duck Island, a remote fishing station close to American waters, when someone near the stern shouted, "Man overboard!" The crew rushed to the back of the boat, but by the time they arrived all they could see was a man's hand reaching out of the water. It took three minutes to turn the *Milton* around and by then, the hand had disappeared. Coming alongside, crew members scooped up a hat and pipe floating on the surface.

The items, it turned out, belonged to Harry Varco, the ship's steward and a popular young man, recently arrived from England. He'd seemed composed enough. Five minutes before, he'd been talking with Captain Crawford in the pilothouse.

Nobody admitted to having seen him fall but the sailors tried to piece together as best they could what had happened. Perhaps Varco had been leaning over the stern watching the propeller when he slipped and fell in. And he must have hit his head, or been sucked in by the churning propeller because otherwise he would have been able to stay above water long enough to be saved. But how could such a strong, capable young man be so careless? There were those who wondered if he'd been angry with the captain and gone aft to blow off steam. The men couldn't stop talking about it. Nobody could.

A memorial service was held at the Wiarton Anglican Church the following Sunday. The pews were packed with Varco's fellow sailors, many of whom were members of the Ancient Order of the Foresters, his fraternal society. They wanted answers. The minister concluded the emotional service by advising that there be an inquest into young Varco's mysterious death. The Forester lodge was willing to begin an investigation immediately. But no one who'd been on board the *Joe Milton* could offer any new information. And none of the boat's crew were willing to swear that they suspected foul play.

It's unclear from newspaper accounts who, exactly, the Anglican minister and the Forester investigators thought could have been responsible. But there's something about the careful way the articles were written and the shroud of silence surrounding the suspicions that makes it sound as if Captain Crawford was a suspect. He, after all, was the last to see Harry Varco alive. Everyone knew he had a stubborn streak as wide as Colpoy's Bay. Perhaps they'd had words. Men who'd sailed with him in the past recalled that he had a temper that could flare unpredictably.

Jim's position as captain and co-owner of the Crawford Tug Company, of course, would have given the men ample reason to keep their mouths shut: if a sailor voiced suspicion, he would be placing himself and his family's livelihood at risk.

In the end, the investigation was dropped. With no family in Canada, Varco's funeral expenses were looked after by his Forester brotherhood.

It must have been a difficult time for Jim Crawford and the tug company. Georgian Bay sailors were a notoriously superstitious bunch. A cat on board, a cross-eyed crew member or rats spotted leaving a vessel were all considered adequate grounds for quitting a boat. And if a steamer or her captain acquired a reputation for being unlucky it was nearly impossible to shake.

It couldn't have helped matters when, less than a month after the Varco drowning, there was a near collision between the *Milton* and the steamer *City of Windsor*. Even though the company was generally well regarded, sailors began watching Old Man Crawford carefully.

The new century also brought tragedy to the Crawfords' own door. In the fall of 1901, Lillie and Jim's fifth child, seventeen-month-old Ada Elizabeth, died. She'd been just starting to run, words—unintelligible but deliberate—burbling out of her tiny upturned lips. Lillie was devastated.

Soon after the little girl died, Lillie discovered that she was expecting again. People told her that the new baby would lift her spirits, but her pregnancy just seemed to intensify her sadness, each swish and kick of the child inside her sending waves of melancholy through her body. When Richard Munroe, who would be known as Dick, was born in the summer of 1902, Lillie continued to tie dark armbands on the other four children. She kept all her jewellery tucked away in little velvet boxes. The glinting white gold and diamonds in her favourite crescent brooch just seemed too garish and sad.

The early 1900s were hard times for many families in Wiarton. The forests north on the peninsula and Manitoulin Island were almost gone and no one had replanted. People were nervous, as everyone in the area depended in some way on either the forests or the fish.

Some of the forward-thinking men on Wiarton council began to look for ways to diversify the town's economy. After numerous ideas were examined and discarded, W. D. Forrest, a local man with a determined look about his eyes and a penchant for invention, managed to convince the town's politicians and merchants that prosperity lay in the sugar beet industry. Northern states as well as nearby towns like Wallaceburg and Dresden had found success in distilling sugar from beets. A manufacturing plant would employ factory workers, skilled workmen and administrators, and offer local farmers a market for their efforts. It might even replace the lumber industry. A successful factory would attract other businesses to town.

During the summer and fall of 1902, people in Wiarton watched as an enormous four-storey building made of limestone faced with brick rose out of nothing on the south shore of Colpoy's Bay. It was bigger than any building on the peninsula. Editors at the newspaper expressed the community's hopes when they wrote that now the little town on the shores of Colpoy's Bay could finally claim its rightful place as *the* City of the North.

But in its first year the sugar beet factory ran up a huge debt. It was hard to find workers trained on the equipment, even harder to get supervisors who could teach the unskilled men. And when the equipment broke down no one knew how to fix it. Barrels full of beets rotted waiting at the docks or in the huge storage sheds.

Still, no one in Wiarton was willing to give up right away. The town council extended the factory a loan. Private citizens were convinced to put up bonds amounting to $110,000. That year, 150 people worked in the refinery's sheds and buildings. It was a good living for the workers, and for much of the season things seemed to be running smoothly. But then the whispers started: the out-of-town manager brought in for his expertise was a fall-down drunk; the plant was utterly inefficient. At the end of the financial year, the company posted another loss. In 1903, the company was forced to declare bankruptcy.

Auction notices began to fill the newspaper. When the bonds were called in to settle the debt, at least one businessman was forced to sell his store and equipment to pay. He moved West to start again. He wasn't the only one. Farmers were probably the hardest hit, with many families forced to sell everything and move away. The CPR offered an excursion rate from the Bruce to Manitoba and the Northwest. One precision-minded citizen of Owen Sound reported counting eighty vacant houses on the streets of Wiarton.

☙❧

April 29, 1905, Wiarton harbour

The crowd on the docks near the Crawford Tug Company sheds is restless. Arrangements for the launch of the new steam tug have taken longer than expected.

There must be two hundred people jostling for a view from the wharf and the dirty, lumber-strewn shore. The little boys who spent long cold winter afternoons watching A. A. Hackett and his men carefully building the steel-framed, oak-panelled steamer are there; so are local merchants, businessmen and every sailor in town. But their enthusiasm is starting to wane. The older ones, especially, have that hangdog look of people who've been standing too long.

Jim Crawford is beginning to get angry. Hackett's been saying for weeks now that the boat would be ready for this morning and now he claims to have last-minute work to do. The well-wishers have been waiting for nearly an hour. Jim has shaken hands with almost everyone, smiled and said it's-going-to-be-any-minute-now countless times, but now he's not so sure. All winter he's let the man set the pace—he's treated him like some sort of artist. But he has finally reached the end of his tether.

He pushes his way into Hackett's shed, the heavy wooden door slamming shut behind him.

"*What* is going on?" he demands, hands on his hips.

"All right, all right, Jim," Hackett says in his calm drawl. "We're ready to go."

Deflated, Jim smoothes down the front of his navy wool coat with one hand. He adjusts his hat. "Good then. Let's proceed. Immediately." He holds the door open.

Hackett and two of his workers leave the shed and disappear up into the boat that sits in a cradle on shore. Wooden blocks hold the timbers underneath in place; they will be hammered away when the steamer is launched, sending the boat sliding into the water. Hackett's men adjust the fitting they'd been working on and climb down within a few minutes.

Jim leaves the boat to find his brother. Jack is talking animatedly to a friend near the end of the dock, apparently oblivious that they are now a full hour off schedule. Jim is half-surprised that Jack is even here, he's been so distracted after buying the old sawmill and timber limits a few weeks ago. The *Echo* reported that it was the largest real estate deal ever transacted on the peninsula.

Together, the Crawford brothers mount the small platform that has been built flush with the boat's deck. The Red Ensign flaps from an improvised mast on board. From their perch overlooking the crowd they can see people shuffling and rubbing their eyes. Jim gives a small wave to his five children standing on the dock with their aunt Susie. It's only Lillie and baby Eleanor who couldn't attend the ceremony; the doctor advised against it since the child is only two days old and Lillie needs her rest. But little Dick is there, squeezed into the old Crawford tartan and matching lace-collared shirt. Ten-year-old Madge is beside him, barely restrained from dashing off with the three older boys and getting her dress dirty in the coal and muck around the sheds. There are some mothers in town who refuse to let their daughters play with the girl, in case her tomboy ways rub off. But Lillie's sister Susie will keep her and the others in line. She is twenty-three and unmarried, a sturdy girl, pleasant enough to look at with that pile of dark, dark hair.

Peering out across Colpoy's Bay Jim can see the sugar beet factory, that hulking advertisement of the town's folly. He'd rather not look at it and angles himself so that his view is of the open water and the leafless grey trees on the southern shore. He doesn't need another reminder of how much both his company and the town need a successful season of navigation, about all that is riding on him, on this new boat. As it is, they're going to be stretched thin this year with seven vessels at work, including this new one and the *Jones*.

Jim gives the musician standing next to him a nod. He's a trumpeter, a local favourite for his ragtime songs. The man breathes deeply and plays a few bars to get the crowd's attention. Then, in a deep, commanding voice that he generally reserves for his crew, Jim welcomes the assembled people. He is pleased, he says, to announce that the brand-new steam tug will be known as the *Crawford*.

Jack raises a pistol into the air to fire a salute. The sound is nearly drowned out by the dull thudding of a hammer against the wooden blocks, then the splinter-ing of timbers as they are compressed by the heavy boat. The vessel moves slowly at first, but gathers speed at the last moment and splashes into the water, rolling back and forth, throwing waves of icicle water on the people gathered nearby. The children on the dock scream their delight.

❦

The *Crawford* quickly proved a welcome addition to the tug company fleet. Her launch gave the Crawford brothers and the town a much-needed boost. But in September, off the tip of Cape Croker, one of the brothers' faithful old tugs, the *A. Seaman*, burned to the waterline. And a week later the roof of the company's large warehouse on the water-front caught fire. The local volunteer fire brigade rushed to the scene, whistles screaming, horses in a lather. The firemen battled a sharp wind blowing from the west, fighting the flames with hose and axe. The blaze was quickly brought under control but it left an enormous hole in the roof of the warehouse.

It would have been small comfort to Jim Crawford as he arranged for the remains of the *Seaman* to be hauled back to the company's damaged warehouse, that Crawford Tug wasn't the only organization that had sustained difficult losses. There had been three big storms that season and by the close of navigation, seventy ships were reported wrecked on Lake Huron. Nearly 150 people died, and there was an accumulated loss of almost $7 million.

It was the steady, reliable *Jones* that kept the Crawfords from losing confidence in those early years of the new century. She was the company's stalwart, the biggest and most important boat in their fleet. No matter what happened with the rest of the tugs and tenders, the *Jones* kept to her usual route, rarely missing a trip. To people in Wiarton, the steamer was an old friend: familiar and obliging. When the *Echo* reported that a travelling theatrical troupe in Owen Sound had made fun of her ear-piercing whistle during a skit, local readers were indignant.

So the news of April 1906 was particularly satisfying: the *Jones* was the first boat of the season into Owen Sound harbour, blowing hard on her whistle all the way down the bay.

The summer that followed was the hottest on record. A store in Wiarton sold ice cream in big solid bricks and every chance they could steal, people staggered down to the docks to feel the breeze off the bay, mopping their necks with cotton handkerchiefs. Hundreds showed up at the harbour for excursions on the *Jones*—so many that people had to be turned away. One dollar for gentlemen, seventy-five cents for ladies. On still nights you could hear the band playing "'Tis the Last Rose of Summer" all the way from the islands at the mouth of the bay.

But the fall of 1906 came in with a snarl, as wicked as the summer was hot. Heavy seas and early snow made life miserable for the sailors. Reports from the central observatory in Toronto predicted that it wasn't going to be over any time soon. A spell of unsettled weather near the end of November would bring severe winds and stormy weather to Georgian Bay.

*There were many boats in Owen Sound harbour the day the
Jones disappeared, but not many dared go out.*

Chapter 7

THE BIG BLOW

WHEN I BEGAN LOOKING into the wreck of the *J. H. Jones* and the life of my great-grandfather, one of the first things I found was a small booklet titled *Wiarton's Great Disaster*. Published by the Bruce County Historical Society in 1972, it's a charming, folksy read relying on the gilded memories of old-timers from the Wiarton docks. There are photographs and a sea shanty about the wreck ("The Steamer Jones of Wiarton lay in Owen Sound's sheltered 'swatch'/Whilst Captain Crawford paced the deck a-fumbling with his watch"). I have pored over the booklet many times since, staring at the images of the captain and his crew, stopping each time at one particularly poignant photograph of the first mate, Edward E. Lennox. The studio portrait of the twenty-three-year-old man was apparently discovered on the shore of Christian Island after the wreck, its corners rubbed off on the rocks but the picture itself clear as day.

Later, I dug up the newspaper accounts published at the time of the disaster and then again five, ten, twenty and thirty-five years later. I found letters to the editor and elegiac poems written by family members of the victims. A lot of it repeated the same facts but there were also many discrepancies.

I've tried to piece it all together, stitching the disparate, sometimes contradictory stories into something resembling a whole. I've dug in archives and libraries, talked to historians and family members of the crew. I've followed red herrings to capture a minor and ultimately unusable detail; I've littered my home with Post-its and paper napkins trying to find links and explanations. But I've discovered that like a family story, the tale of the *Jones* is messy and incomplete. Even with all these mounds of paper, with all the stories from people who remembered the boat and her crew, with eyewitness accounts of her departure and passage and the accumulated wisdom of nearly a century, it will never be quite finished. For there were no survivors, no one to tell the real story of what happened that cold November afternoon.

November 22, 1906, 10 a.m., Owen Sound harbour

John Macaulay edges his way past a trio of deckhands stacking a pile of lumber on the dock, dodges two horse-drawn cutters—careful not to brush against the dirty metal of the sleigh—and walks up the stern gangplank to look for the *Jones*'s first mate. He'd like passage home to Wiarton and she's the quickest way there.

Despite the blustering wind, the air is heavy with the scent of coal oil and fish. Macaulay's worked on the docks most of his life but he's always disliked the clammy smells. He tries not to breathe through his nose.

There are a lot of boats in harbour, though not many are venturing out. With the fishing season finished, some of the smaller tugs are already up on dry dock for the winter. Macaulay will be glad for the end of navigation this year. It's been a miserable fall. Snow squalls and crackling cold. But there's still nearly a month before the ice comes in and any captain with something to carry will keep busily at it. Nobody can afford to be choosy in times like these.

The *Caribou*, the newest and largest of Macaulay's boats in the Dominion fleet, had a close call just two weeks ago. A sudden gale nearly sank her off Cape Croker. Huge, rolling waves caused the cargo of fish boxes to shift in her hold, making the boat hard to control. Waves broke over her upper deck, Captain Batten told Macaulay, and he thought he'd finally taken his last trip on the Turkey Trail.

Macaulay laughed at him just a bit. Batten's a good master, an excellent navigator, but notorious for his caution.

Each fall he'll lose an hour or two one day waiting out the weather, then a full day here and there until, by the end of the season, he's late a full week—and right back on schedule. He'll be especially careful now. But at least he always comes through. And in the brutal storms this time of year, it's more than you can say about some.

Macaulay has been through so many fall seasons, he's lost count. He usually likes it. The way the golden light can make even the most ordinary things beautiful. The unpredictable predictability of it all: bad weather, then clear red and yellow days, then bad weather again. Up on the Bustard Islands when he was just a boy starting out, it was so barren and rocky and open it felt like you were a part of the storm. He'd watch the winter weather coming in, waves piling up, water spraying the air like fireworks.

Macaulay pokes his head into the *Jones's* wheelhouse. The first mate, Ed Lennox, isn't there. Nobody is. Macaulay allows himself a moment to linger in the little room. He knows it like his own hand. Just big enough for three men standing close together, the space is utilitarian, with nowhere to sit. In front, there's a big polished wooden wheel, a barometer, compass, the old clock and a place to lay out charts.

It's getting late. He steps back over the wheelhouse's raised door frame and walks along the side toward the stern, past small passenger cabins on one side, the water on the other. He begins to run his hand along the low metal railing but it's shockingly cold and he lifts his hand away with a jerk. He leans into one of the cabins where the door is open. Nobody there. He finally spots Lennox supervising some deckhands loading lumber through the forward gangway at the side of the boat.

"Good morning, sir," Lennox says, unfolding his long body to face the older man.

"Morning, Lennox. I'd like passage to Wiarton."

The tall, thin first mate shakes his head. His cheeks are flushed and pink, which makes him look even younger than he is. "Sorry, Mr. Macaulay, sir, but she's not stopping in. She's expected in Lion's Head, then Tobermory tomorrow."

Macaulay frowns, patting down the dark hair at the back of his head and rubbing his neck. He'll have to take the train, wait in Park Head for an hour and half. He'll be late for supper.

Cursing his bad luck and the Grand Trunk Railway, Macaulay nods to Lennox and leaves the *Jones*, calling out hello to Captain Jim, whom he spots from a distance. Jim pulls out his watch at the end of a long chain and taps the glass at his old friend. He's late, and if Macaulay knows him at all, not too happy about it.

10:15 a.m., Owen Sound harbour

Alex Lyons's dark serge suit is crushed after his long trip. It's the one he had made in Whitehorse, the one he's worn since he left the Yukon two weeks ago. He figured he would look like a man about town in it, figured his mother and brother Fred would be impressed with what he's made of himself after all those years up north. But now it's wrinkled and his hat looks like a horse trampled it.

Alex feels a bit trampled himself after a close call on the way down the coast to Vancouver. The ship he took passage on had seemed sturdy, not especially old or overloaded. But the wind was tremendous, the waves like no breakers he'd seen growing up in Owen Sound. He'd kissed the dock when they pulled into Vancouver harbour. Then a couple of days later he picked up the *Daily Province* and read on the front page that the boat he'd been on sank on its return trip. People had died. People that could have been him.

But as he sets out from the train station to look for his older brother, Alex feels more brave than frightened. He's had some time to digest his near miss. He'll surprise Fred with his early arrival. Go see him at his new restaurant.

Alex walks slowly into town, taking in everything that has changed in Owen Sound. There are two automobiles on Russell Street alone—more than there were in the whole town when he left. Shiny metal boxes with fat wheels, the paint so brilliant you could comb your hair in it. And there are many new shops. He tips his hat at two girls who pass by and giggle at him. Alex finds his brother sweeping the sidewalk outside the restaurant. Fred was a checker at the CPR sheds when Alex left Owen Sound, but he's come up in the world since. He's just opened this eatery at the corner of Russell and Marsh Streets. It has electric lights.

The brothers shake hands, then awkwardly embrace. Then, as if possessed by his younger self, as if he hasn't just returned from four years of being a man on his own terms in the Yukon district, the first thing Alex does is relay his terrifying story, spitting it out like a plug of tobacco onto the dusty road. Fred leans on his broom as they talk and nods in all the right places, patting his brother on the back when he pauses to catch his breath.

Fred tells him that he knows something about shipwrecks after working his entire adult life near the docks. He says he understands Alex's terror. He's seen his share of boats going out and never coming back. But what Fred figures Alex needs, what any man needs in such a circumstance, is a bit of the hair of the dog that bit him. If he is planning to come home to Owen Sound to stay, it won't do to be afraid of boats. Their mother is headed up to Lion's Head for a visit that afternoon, and Alex can go with her. A quick nip up the coast, no more than a couple of hours on the water, the wind of Georgian Bay blowing on his face and Alex will be good as new. Shipshape, Fred says. But they'll have to hurry. It's nearly past boarding time for the *Jones*.

The Lyons brothers leave Alex's bags at the restaurant and half run, half walk over to the Crawford Tug Company boat. They see red-faced deckhands still rushing back and forth between the docks and the boat's open gangways, steam from their breath like a cloud around the boat. There's still a lot of freight on the docks. Lumber and sacks of flour, crates of apples, pails of lard.

Alex spots his mother before she sees him. She's sitting on a wooden bench just beyond the fray, a small fabric bag at her feet. Her cheeks look like two shiny Macintoshes, and she's rubbing her gloved hands together to keep warm. Alex runs over and stops in front of her. When she looks up she lets out a yelp. The dock workers pause momentarily in the echo of her cry, staring dully at mother and son. But by then Mrs. Lyons is hugging Alex and then Fred and then Alex again. She's been waiting for this moment for four years and isn't going to pretend she didn't miss her boy. She told everyone she felt ripped in two when he left.

It's bad enough that she's alone and Fred is so busy all the time, but with Alex in the Yukon she thought she'd never enjoy another thing again. Now here he is and the thick November clouds might just slide aside and pour warm marmalade sunshine on them all.

Pulling away from his mother, Alex straightens his jacket and his necktie. "I'll have to get a ticket," he says in a deep voice that does nothing to disguise his pleasure. "Will you wait for me here, Mother?"

Alex lines up behind two women who are taking turns soothing a baby. The child's face is contorted, as if it's momentarily stopped breathing. But then it inhales and opens its perfect pink mouth to let out a high-pitched wail. Alex smiles half-heartedly at the two women and shuffles his feet. Once they've bought their tickets, he advances up the line. The agent says the *Jones* is running late.

Alex buys a round-trip ticket and heads back toward his mother. He wonders how best to tell her that he very nearly died. He doesn't want to worry her. As he settles onto the bench, he tries not to think about the cold wind or the frantic beating of the canvas weather cloth around the *Jones's* hurricane deck.

❦

11 a.m., Owen Sound

Once the boat is loaded, it takes the *Jones* twenty more minutes to get up steam. John Macaulay watches from shore as the final passengers embark. Soon, smoke billows from the steamer's tall, raked stack and the *Jones* begins to pull away from the dock. The snow coming down is swallowed by the water.

But instead of heading out into the bay, the *Jones* moves just across the harbour. The already heavily laden steamer pulls up at the Queen City Oil Company berths.

There the crew rolls some twenty barrels of coal oil onto the upper deck near a brick-making machine already stowed there. Normally, the men would place the barrels upright but—Macaulay can't help noticing—in the rush to get out of port they lash them together and leave them on their sides.

It's nearly an hour past the *Jones*'s regular sailing time, and the boat is still at the oil docks when Macaulay spots Art Batten steering the *Caribou* into harbour. He stifles a smile as he watches the new boat negotiate the harbour like a boxer dancing on the waves. But, suddenly, Macaulay sees Batten alter course, pulling astern of the *Jones*. His steamer glazed with sleet and wind, Batten steps out of the *Caribou*'s wheelhouse and calls to Captain Jim to wait.

From the other side of the river Macaulay sees Captain Batten climb aboard the *Jones* and stride purposefully down the deck. When he gets to the wheelhouse, Batten disappears for a moment. All of a sudden, he emerges again, stomping back and up onto his own vessel. He signals to his wheelsman to head to the *Caribou*'s berth at the Dominion docks.

Intrigued, Macaulay watches the *Jones*'s crew finish loading the oil barrels. When they're done, they release the lines quickly and the boat pushes off, moving through the harbour toward the bay. It's not yet noon but the sky is already dark. The boat seems heavy and low in the water.

When the *Caribou* is safely tied up at the Dominion docks, Macaulay climbs on board to ask about what happened with Old Man Crawford. Batten looks tired. He sighs and shakes his head.

"I told Jim that heavy seas are running out in the bay. Waves breaking nearly twenty-five feet," he says. "I told him to wait it out, but he wouldn't listen."

Macaulay shrugs. "Crawford's a stubborn man," he says. "He'll suit himself."

12:30 p.m., Georgian Bay

Sitting on a bench on the stern deck, Isaac Ackerman has a good view of the other passengers on the *Jones*. Some are strolling, a few are gathered at the very back watching the land disappear behind them. At least one man looks familiar. Donalds or Donaldson. A well-dressed American who works for a fish company in town. Isaac has done business with him. The two men nodded to one another but haven't spoken. And there are three young men he overheard talking about working up on Manitoulin Island for the winter. Loggers probably—they have that lean, scratchy look even though they're dressed in suits. One of them had his nose in a pocket dictionary. Two years ago Isaac might have walked right up to that young man and struck up a conversation. He might have made a friend, shared a flask, talked about horses or the future of automobiles or where to get a good pair of boots. But now he feels old. So much has changed for him in such a short amount of time. It's hard to know what to say, hard to talk to strangers when you can't think of words to make sense of it all even to yourself.

Isaac stamps his feet on the deck to stay warm. He grips the front panels of his wool coat in each hand and pulls them forcefully across his body. He can see the trees on shore leaning over in the wind. The snow is coming down hard now.

A young man and an older woman, who is obviously his mother, quickly walk by, headed for the relative warmth of the cabin. The man is solid-looking, wearing a dark, lumpy jacket, and the woman has her hand stuck proudly through his arm. She might as well be on a promenade. The young man, too, has a confident gait, deliberate, as if he knows exactly what's in front of him.

Isaac forces himself to look away. He doesn't want them to see him watching. Breathing deeply, he tucks his chin into the collar of his coat and lowers his eyes. He feels a lump rising in his throat.

It's thinking about his own mother that makes him feel like this. The sacrifices she made for him. He hasn't even seen her in more than two years. She could very well be dead right now and he wouldn't even know it.

She was the one who'd convinced him to leave Warsaw and the Russian army. They'd have been more than happy to kill a Jew if he took a wrong step. She'd arranged everything. He went into a particular tavern, and when the other men were drunk he slipped out the back door. From there it was twenty miles across country to the cellar of an acquaintance where he hid out until the search cooled off. When they'd given up on him entirely, he hitched a ride across the German frontier and then sailed to England.

Her plan had worked perfectly, except that England was wet and cold. And it was small; surrounded so closely by water, the country made him restless. Though he was trained as a tinsmith, he couldn't find work and felt that he was always under suspicion—for his face, his foreign tongue. He couldn't go back to Poland so he decided he might as well go to Canada. The country was vast, he'd heard, and even a poor man could afford land.

Isaac has a friend who helps him write letters home to Warsaw, but he hasn't heard back from his mother and sister in a long while. Anything might have happened. He tries not to think about it. Watching the mother and son walking together on the deck he can almost feel his own mother's big soft hands cradling his face, the quick, embarrassed squeeze his sister gave him just before he fled.

He wishes he could talk to them and tell them he's met some other Jews, that he even observed Yom Kippur in September. About sixty Owen Sound people rented out a big room in a tenement building at Scopes and Division Streets. They came from as far away as Kincardine and Lion's Head.

He wants them to hear how well he's doing at his new business. People in Montreal told him when he arrived in Canada that there are only two options for a Jew: junk dealing or working in one of the Jewish stores. It didn't sound like much of an option at the time but it turned out that the junk business suits him. He likes that he has a chance to move around a lot, that he runs his own show. And there's no end to the junk—rags and rubbers, glass, bones, horse hair, wool pickings, sheep skins, metal scrap. He's headed today to Cockburn Island to get a big heap of iron that he'll unload later. He's heard there are metal companies down in Toronto and Hamilton who might want him as their point man on the peninsula.

3 p.m., south of Cape Croker

Through the tiny window in the passenger dining area, Richard Addison watches nervously as the sky begins to turn black. He pats the pocket dictionary he's just tucked into his suit jacket. He can feel the reassuring outline of the tiny book—its familiar tattered cover and water-bloated pages—through the rough material.

Richard has always been jittery on the water and now, since the first mate demanded all passengers go inside and stay there, it's all he can do to breathe deeply and watch the horizon. Some of the other passengers have gone to their staterooms on the upper deck but many people have gathered in the dining area. They are shivering and whispering in the small, wood-panelled space.

Richard is glad he's wearing a life preserver, even if it is uncomfortable and he had to pester the young mate a couple of times to get it for him. It makes him feel better to know he has it fastened tightly around his waist. Just in case.

If he didn't have to, he'd never set foot on a boat again. This time, he'd had to leave Manitoulin to recruit new loggers for the camp where he works during the winter. As his father used to say, he doesn't have to like it, but he has to do it all the same.

Logging is no picnic, either. The work is hard. Dangerous, even. Sometimes the men and the boss are likeable enough; other times it's an angry, fighting crew. There's almost no way to predict it because nobody's the same after a couple of months in the bush. Everything can be going well, and then someone will sneak in liquor or he won't get a letter from his girl and the whole place changes because of this one man's misery. This year Richard has persuaded his little brother, Ed, and their cousin to come up with him. They're over in the corner trying unsuccessfully to sleep. He hopes they aren't regretting their decision already.

Richard can see through the window that the waves are mounting. Despite the darkness there's a strange luminescence in the air. It's making the water look a murky glowing grey-blue, while white crests appear and disappear, sucked under by the waves. The *Jones* is bouncing up and down, the bow crashing off the top of a wave into the trough of the sea, then rising again.

Some of the passengers have been seasick and there's the unmistakable stench of vomit in the room. Everyone looks pale. There's a group huddled together near the single coal lamp. A few of the younger men are sitting on the floor and some of the ladies have found an uncomfortable seat on the hard, wooden benches. It's too turbulent for the cook to make the noonday meal they'd been promised, but earlier he had come out of the galley with a large loaf of hard bread. The passengers who can bear to eat pass it around and saw off slices with a heavy knife.

The worse the rolling and pitching gets, the less people talk to one another. But there's one well-dressed man with a club bag at his feet who can't seem to keep quiet. Richard hears him announce in the kind of voice that commands everyone's attention that he travels on the *Jones* a lot.

"This is nothing," he gamely tells the other passengers. "Not compared to the storms last year. There were waves then that could topple a Chicago skyscraper."

Richard knows the man's bravado is meant to inspire confidence but talk of other storms just makes him more nervous. He tries to block out the man's voice and concentrate on the words he read in his dictionary waiting for the *Jones* to be loaded.

"Cerulean. Cerulean. Cerulean." Richard faces the window and whispers his new word over and over to himself to take possession of the soft consonants and long vowels. "Resembling the blue of the sky." It's like a song. It makes him think of another day, a couple of months before, when he'd stolen away for a catnap in a field dense with yellow wheat. He'd lain there for a while, still awake, his muscles throbbing from working the threshing machine. He'd been mesmerized by the summer sky, the buzz of the cicadas, the changing shapes jumping out of passing clouds. Cerulean blue.

The boat crashes down again and Richard grabs at the wall for balance. Through the window, he can see water pressing against the glass. The boat seems to hover there, bow deep in the water, stern waving in the air. Cups and saucers crash off the tables and an old woman who was sitting in the corner with her daughter and grandchild falls off her seat and slides down the floor toward the bow. A chair goes skidding after her. The lady screams as she falls, tangled in her skirts and coat.

Then, just as abruptly, the *Jones* is level, and oddly still. Richard can hear the grumble of the boiler but there's a quiet that wasn't there before. For a second no one gets up to help the old woman. It's as if they are all frozen, their eyes round and unblinking. Then the woman's grandchild lets out a loud cry that fractures the silence, sending words flying in all directions. The talkative man in the dark suit jumps up to help the old woman to her feet. He speaks to her as he offers his hand and she groans and nods impatiently. *Yes, yes.*

People are talking loudly now. The old woman's family is on their knees facing the wall, praying. Richard looks over at his younger brother. He's trying to appear calm but Richard can tell by the way Ed is clenching his teeth, straining the muscles in his neck, that he's frightened now. Ed had scoffed loudly at his older brother's insistence on a life preserver. It's a small, neatly parcelled, sibling kind of triumph that he isn't scoffing now.

3:15 p.m., Cape Croker lighthouse

The sound of the big slabs of limestone sliding back and forth at the shore makes lighthouse keeper Richard Chapman's teeth ache. If he thinks about it, which he does even though he resents such stray musings flitting unbidden through his mind, it reminds him of his old schoolhouse back in England and how some of the children tormented others with the sound of their fingernails raking down the chalkboard. The crunching of the rock in the waves is like that. It hits him first in the jaw and then in the back of his mouth, throwing dull spears through his skull.

It's nearly always windy at the lighthouse but it takes a big blow to whip the water into a force that can move the limestone. As soon as the boy woke him that morning Chapman knew that it was going to be one of those days. It was nasty and dark and sometime mid-morning the waves started rising up, curling off the rocks at the beach, spraying his little compound. Pellets of snow beat against the glass of the light. Chapman doesn't usually turn the light on until sunset, but at one o'clock he decided that any sailors brave or foolish enough to be out in this storm would welcome the roving flash and the sound of the foghorn.

When Chapman spots the *J. H. Jones* out past Hay Island to his south she looks to be holding up well, considering the weather. At 3:30 p.m. Chapman scribbles in his log that the *Jones* has passed the lighthouse. He can see more swell than boat at times but she's going eight or nine knots, a good speed for the wind. He peers out from the watch room as Captain Jim battles the waves toward Cove of Cork Bay. He won't have a problem making the turn into Lion's Head.

Relaxing his vigil Chapman realizes he's been watching so hard his eyes are burning. He doesn't want to lose sight of the *Jones* until he is certain she'll make port. He knows he can't prevent the vessels that pass his lighthouse from getting into trouble, but sometimes he thinks that if he watches them closely, if he never looks away, the force of his attention will keep them from harm. Once a boat sails within sight of Lion's Head to the north or Griffith Island to the south he relinquishes responsibility to the keepers there.

Chapman steps backwards down the narrow ladder inside the tower, holding the low wooden banister. This weather always makes him feel old, his joints brittle, like veneer starting to crack. His young helper can stand watch while he has a cup of tea to warm up. It's easy work now that they've got the electric light and foghorn. The first in the county, he reminds the boy often.

Sipping tea in the house next to the tower Chapman watches the wind move over the water, lifting it into peaks of cold spray. It's impressive, in the way that the flames of a bonfire can be, all the dangerous potential forgotten in watching its strange whimsy. But the storm seems to be dying out. The wind is starting to slow. Instead of crashing, the waves collapse; they fall in on themselves, then rise again like vanquished prizefighters struggling off the mat.

After twenty-five years on Georgian Bay, Jim Crawford (front, centre) was too experienced to ignore the signs in the sky the day he and his crew set off on their final voyage.

Chapter 8

RED SKY IN THE MORNING

IT IS DIFFICULT for anyone who hasn't seen Georgian Bay in full flight to fully comprehend its fury. The weather can change dramatically hour to hour, even minute to minute. It is a lake but it can act with the power of an ocean.

Spending summers at Pointe au Baril and, later, sailing along the east and northern shore in a thirty-three-foot sailboat my baby-boomer parents anointed *Peacetrain*, I have learned respect for Georgian Bay. I love its moods and intensity. But I also fear it. The water is cold, bearable only for a few weeks in July and August. It rises and falls, whole islands emerging and just as suddenly disappearing into the blue; shoals can appear where once there was unperturbed water. The winds are shifty and capricious.

When we were sailing on *Peacetrain* during storms or under questionable skies, the VHF radio would always be tuned in to the weather channel of what was then known as Wiarton Coast Guard Radio "serving Lake Huron and Georgian Bay." Often I'd go below into the small cabin to hear the familiar buzzing Scottish voice: "Marine forecast issued at 04:00. Lake Huron, Georgian Bay, winds northwest thirty diminishing to fifteen by noon, to light and variable in the afternoon. Waves two metres, subsiding. . ."

To call through to the station my mother or father would switch frequencies and talk into the mouthpiece: "Wiarton Coast Guard Radio, Wiarton Coast Guard Radio, Wiarton Coast Guard Radio, this is *Peacetrain*, *Peacetrain*, *Peacetrain*." You could hear others doing the same. Mostly it was sailors asking for news about water levels or reporting a buoy that was missing or a light out. Sometimes there'd be a distress call, someone who'd seen a waterspout or storm tide, a boat that hit a shoal or ran out of fuel. Once we listened as a terrified person reported "man overboard." We could hear the panic in the caller's voice, the wind whistling across the mouthpiece. People all over the bay would have been glued to the VHF to hear the outcome. In those tense moments it felt as if a thin line separated me and my family from those pleading for rescue.

But we sailed mostly in the summer—the calmest and warmest time on Georgian Bay. Anyone who knows the Great Lakes will tell you that it is the autumn that you need to watch. The gales of November have been enshrined in song and myth, their suddenness and force unrivalled the rest of the year. It is the month when the Lake Superior ore carrier *Edmund Fitzgerald* famously went down with all hands in 1975. It is when the *Jane Miller* sank in 1881, the *Algoma* in 1885, the *Bannockburn* in 1902, and it is when, in a matter of a few days, the Great Storm of 1913 wrecked forty boats and took the lives of 235 sailors on Lake Huron alone.

There have been no major fall shipwrecks on the Great Lakes since the *Fitzgerald* sank, but in the early days of the twentieth century, each November the captains and crews of the wooden steamers prepared themselves for news of lost boats. Racing against the weather, they hoped they'd get lucky and outrun the storms. Spray off the water would turn to ice, coating the wooden decks and making the trip from bow to stern a slippery, dangerous ride. And loaded down with ice, the boats were heavy and low in the water, hard to control. Sailors worked day and night to get in as many trips as possible; the crew stuck by the Old Man to get an end-of-the-season bonus and ensure a job for the spring.

Marine insurance on Georgian Bay often ran out by the beginning of November in those days, but most captains and owners couldn't afford to put too much weight on the cold feet of insurance men. Freight fees and passenger rates were simply raised to compensate. Any boat with cargo to haul would keep running until the ice chased her out of the bay.

Sailors found comfort in omens and hunches, in signals from the wind and sky. Those with a "weather eye" were revered for their alertness to changes in the patterns of the wind, for their steady confidence in what they could feel in their bones. But any sailor who'd been on the water for a season learned to recognize signs in the heavens. There was folklore for every forecast.

Mackerel sky and mares' tails, make tall ships dowse lofty sails.

*Red sky at night, sailor's delight. Red sky in the morning,
   sailors take warning.*

They would watch the soot in their fireplaces ("When soot begins to fall, the weather soon will squall"), the morning dew ("When dew is on the grass, rain will never come to pass") and count the chirps of the black field cricket. Tested over centuries and across continents, these weather sayings were trusted; they were used in concert with whatever technology was available to make important decisions about when to sail, where to go and when to stay in port.

Instinct and folklore was nearly as good as weather forecasting got in those days. It wasn't the technology that was the problem—the central weather observatory in Toronto was actually quite accurate in its predictions—the issue was the lack of reliable communication between the observatory and more remote areas. There were still people who remembered when farmers living in the Windsor to Halifax corridor could watch the passing trains for weather information. A large metal full moon attached to the front of the engine or side of the baggage cars meant sunny weather, a crescent moon indicated rain, a star prolonged showers.

By the 1900s, probability sheets, which detailed the weather forecast for a twenty-four-hour period, were being sent each day except Sunday from the observatory to telegraph offices in small towns across eastern Canada.

The "probs," as they were known, were meant to be posted on the outside of public buildings. But the information didn't always arrive in time to be useful, or workers didn't bother posting them. And even when they saw the forecast, a lot of old-timers, especially the prickly sailing masters of the Great Lakes, figured they probably knew more about the inland seas than some pointy-head in Toronto.

Once out on the water, sailors were on their own, anyway. There was no ship-to-shore radio or VHF weather channel to transmit the news. A steamer captain relied on his barometer, compass and anemometer to measure wind speed but, mostly, he relied on his judgment.

With nearly twenty-five years of sailing on Georgian Bay, Jim Crawford was too experienced a master to ignore the signs in the sky the morning he set out on his last voyage. He would have consulted his barometer and measured the wind speed, talked to other captains. Perhaps he checked the soot in his fireplace, too. But there were also other, non-weather-related factors he had to take into account: he almost certainly felt pressure to complete the last run of the *Jones's* season. There was business to finish; his crew wanted to get home.

So did he see something in the sky that made him decide it would be safe to leave Owen Sound in stormy seas with a heavy load of passengers and freight? Or did he simply weigh his options and calculate that he and the *Jones* were up for the challenge of the blowing snow and gathering wind? Was he cocky or stupid or just unlucky that day?

I took my questions with me one cold spring morning when I trekked up to the Environment Canada library on a particularly desolate stretch in the northern reaches of Toronto. Housed on the second floor of a government-issue concrete bunker of a building, the library has an impressive archive of documents, maps and journals about weather, some of which go as far back as the 1850s. With the guidance and calm enthusiasm of meteorologist Geoff Coulson, I was able to track the course of the storm that the *Jones* encountered. The way Coulson described the movement of the weather in those late-November days of 1906 was like the plot of a particularly dark and foreboding novel.

The language meteorologists use to describe storms and air masses is, in fact, unabashedly literary—imbued with the flavour of its folkloric past, touched by the drama of the events it describes. A rapidly moving storm sailing eastward from the western provinces is known as a "prairie schooner." The centre of a low pressure system is described as "riding a wave" of warm and cold air. The dividing line between two air masses is a "front," as if it were a war between two competing temperatures. And, in fact, the way meteorologists see it, the constant movement of the weather—rising and falling, clashing and abating—is like a battle.

According to Coulson, the story of the storm that hit the *Jones* begins at least two days before it arrived on the Bruce Peninsula. Interpreting the cryptic undulations and symbols on a weather map of the northern hemisphere, he could see that though it was only partly cloudy with light winds and seasonal temperatures on Georgian Bay, there was weather brewing in Arkansas and Mississippi. A low pressure system was gathering force and heading north-ward. The American Midwest, lower Michigan and southwestern Ontario were already experiencing snow and rain, though the wind wasn't especially strong.

But by 8 o'clock the next morning, the day before the *Jones* left Owen Sound, the weather had changed considerably. Nearby Muskoka was reporting gusts reaching fifteen knots and Lake Superior was experiencing even stronger winds. The low pressure system had shot up to the north over central Illinois, just southwest of Chicago, and was butting against a ridge of high pressure anchored over southern Quebec. Thermal contrast is the engine of any storm and by the evening of November 21, 1906, the stage was set for a massive clash over Lake Huron and Georgian Bay.

The reason autumn is so brutal on the Great Lakes is that as the days get shorter and the weather colder, the contrast between the warm and cold air masses meeting over the lakes becomes very dramatic. Canada's Arctic air and the warm, moist air masses from the United States collide, creating the kind of energy demanded by big, intense storms. Add to this the fact that the Great Lakes are still relatively warm in the fall, providing heat and moisture to the approaching storms, and you've got an explosive situation.

At about 2 a.m. on November 22, 1906, the storm hit its height. With blowing snow and thirty- to forty-knot gale force winds, visibility would have been extremely restricted, with waves in the open beginning to build into mountains of water.

With thirty-knot winds, waves on Georgian Bay can be substantial. In general, the longer and faster the wind blows from a single direction, the bigger the waves. The danger for sailors is that the power of the wind to produce waves and push a boat around does not increase linearly, but as the *square* of the velocity. Which means that a ten-knot wind is not twice, but four times as powerful as a five-knot breeze. When that ten-knot blow picks up to thirty knots, it becomes nine times as strong. This exponential increase is translated to the waves.

Sailors call a thirty-four- to forty-knot wind a fresh gale. On land, branches will snap off trees and you have to lean into the wind to make any headway. On the water, waves mount and break into spindrift, shooting foam in streaks like lightning.

But there are other factors in addition to wind strength that determine a wave's height and character. Wind shifts, current, cliff effects and the water's depth also play a role. On the ocean, waves tend to be higher than on the Great Lakes because they have the chance to build up over a much larger and deeper body of water. But waves on the (relatively) shallow lakes can be even more vicious, since they are short and steep, and made more treacherous by the presence of shoals and the interference of islands and other land forms. These sorts of waves are particularly dangerous for relatively small boats like the 107-foot *Jones*. If you throw a wind shift into the mix, causing waves to race across each other from different directions, the bay can be terrifyingly chaotic. When the walls of water hit a boat one after another from every direction, it can feel like you're in a floating punching bag.

By 8 o'clock on the morning of November 22, when the weather map for that day was created, the storm was still battering Georgian Bay. It was cloudy with intermittent snow squalls. But Coulson saw something on the map that I hadn't seen or heard about before. When Jim Crawford and his crew took their weather readings that morning, they would have noticed that the barometer was rising. Better weather appeared to be on its way. With the wind shifting from the west to northwest, they must have deduced that the storm, which had reached fever pitch the previous night, was headed out of the bay. It must have looked as if the worst was over.

But for Jim Crawford and the passengers and crew of the *Jones*, it clearly wasn't. The storm might have been passing but it wasn't gone. It takes several hours for waves as high as twenty feet to die down, especially if they've built up over a long time over a big stretch of water. And the wind shift to the northwest meant that when the boat left the shelter of the peninsula at Cape Croker, they would hit the roughest, biggest sort of waves. The cliffs there make it an especially gusty spot. Waves would hit them from both the west and the northwest, the latter gathering strength and height as they travelled nearly the entire length of Georgian Bay. If the oil barrels or some other heavy cargo shifted as the wind and water battered the boat, it would be next to impossible to control the heavy steamer. It would all be over in a few minutes.

November 22, 1906, 4 p.m., Georgian Bay

Captain Jim has to make a decision. Fast. They've just passed the Cape Croker lighthouse and the seas are looking confused. They're already taking water over the deck, spraying up to the hurricane deck. And the sleet and snow coming down like a drill makes it difficult to make sense of anything.

Willie Ross, the wheelsman, senses the captain's hesitation. "Let's keep 'er running just off the wind," he says. They are huddled close together in the wheelhouse, for warmth as much as want of space, and Jim can feel the young man's hot breath on his cheek. "We'll miss the Head tonight but I don't think we can risk taking 'em beam-to."

"No," Jim nods. "But I don't want to be caught in the open much longer. I wouldn't have left this morning if I didn't think we could make the turn into the Head. We'll pick a smooth wave and turn through."

Willie grumbles to himself as he waits for the Old Man's instructions. Jim counts the waves beginning with a large one. It's difficult to do because of the confused sea, but the seventh and eleventh are usually the largest waves; the ones that follow the smoothest—and smallest. He braces himself with his hands against the door of the wheelhouse. A big wave washes over the deck, plunging the *Jones* low in the water. Jim breathes deeply and gives the signal to Willie. He pulls the brass handle four times to tell the engineer to go full throttle as they turn through the wind. They've done this a hundred times before. The *Jones* alters course bound for Lion's Head.

But the pummelling is worse once they've turned off the wind. The waves are even steeper. Taking them on her starboard bow the *Jones* can't plough through anymore, not when the waves are almost a quarter the length of the entire boat. They're coming quickly, too, three at a time.

Willie holds the wheel firmly as the bow of the boat climbs up the face of a wave and then crashes over the top, coming down into the trough with a thud, like land-ing on concrete. There are moments when it feels to both of them as if they are riding on top of these waves, balanc-ing for a split second, stern out of the water. The tension goes out of the wheel then and it's impossible to steer with the propeller spinning in the air. When the prop again grasps water, Willie struggles against the sudden force of the waves pushing the boat sideways. They both know that if they go beam-to into the trough of the sea, taking the waves directly on their side, the *Jones* will flip over like a dinghy.

Suddenly, Ed Lennox, the first mate, appears in the side window. He's crouched low, clinging to the side of the cabin. When he pulls the narrow door open it snaps vio-lently back, smashing the side of the wheelhouse.

"The cargo has shifted, sir," Ed yells over the wind. "When we turned toward the Head. I've got the deck-hands trying to stabilize her but it's hard to do in these waves. We might need to pitch some over."

Although he has to shout to be heard, Lennox's voice is level. He looks calm enough, though he stands with his long body bent, bracing himself against the weather. He seems unaware that he is shivering. With a thin, muscular forearm, he wipes away the spray that drips from his face.

"Put as many men on it as necessary," says the captain. "And be at the ready. I may need you."

Ed nods and turns to go. He has to lean his whole body on the door to close it. Just as he gets it shut a wave washes over the foredeck. The water shoves him backwards and he grips the side of the cabin and the rail that wraps around the deck.

Inside the wheelhouse, Willie and Jim can feel the cargo on the upper deck move violently with this last wave, a sudden heaving motion that forces the boat to list to port. The one coal lamp flickers, then goes out entirely.

The darkness in the small room is blinding. When his eyes adjust, Willie finds he can barely see the compass. And the *Jones* isn't obeying her helm. Willie spreads his legs wide to get better leverage on the wheel and curses under his breath. They've done this trip so many times they could do it backwards and upside down. He grits his teeth and squints into the dark.

Jim is concentrating on the compass and his own breathing when a white shape leaps out of the pitch, sweeps the deck and explodes into the wheelhouse. Both men try to duck but water slices at their faces and chests like a knife. Icy fingers of water drip down Jim's back.

He blinks. Everything is white. He runs a hand across his eyes and he can see Willie reeling beside him. The front panes and one of the side windows are broken; glass covers them both and sloshes in the water that's up to their knees. Freezing spray blasts the little room.

"You all right?" Jim shouts.

"Yep," Willie gulps.

But nothing is all right. The *Jones* is wallowing. Water is coming in. There's no tension in the wheel. The captain's forehead is bleeding. Jim tries one door but the wind has nailed it shut. When he squeezes past Willie to push the other, it catches the wind and swings open again. Water pours out but there's still half a foot trapped by the raised door frame, and more coming in all the time.

Wesley Sadler, the second engineer, appears red-faced and breathless in the doorway. "We're taking on water, sir. It's in the engine room. We can't keep up steam," he shouts.

Sadler seems feral, like a cat ready to pounce. He looks impatiently to the captain for orders but Jim says nothing. His eyes are half-closed, his moustache drips. There is blood trickling down the side of his face and smeared across his forehead.

"Are the pumps at full force?" he asks finally.

"Aye, sir. But they won't do the job," Sadler spits. The boat is listing now. Jim turns and looks the second engineer in the eye.

"Tell Ed to ready the passengers and lifeboats. Set the flares."

It's a decision no captain wants to make but there is no other choice. The *Jones* is now leaning to port so much that Willie and Jim have to hold the starboard side of the cabin to keep upright. They have almost no steam. They're at the mercy of the storm.

The next wave shrieks through the wheelhouse as if shredding the air. The *Jones* twists as the wave rolls her over. Willie and Captain Jim are thrown off their feet. Stunned, they try to clamber up but a wave pushes them back and Jim loses sight of Willie in the confusion. Water is everywhere. It's unimaginably cold. Fighting frantically for air, Jim grabs onto something he thinks is the door frame of the wheelhouse and tries to drag himself out of the water. He manages to get his head out for a moment and he sputters and coughs, his chest tight, like someone is sitting on it. It's hard to breathe. Then another wave smashes down on him like a hammer. The suction of the sinking boat pulls him deeper and deeper, tugging at his heavy boots and coat. Jim tries to resist, but his body won't obey. Everything seems to happen in half speed. He watches as barrels, apples and bags of flour spiral downward with him.

WRECK OF THE STEAMER

JONES

"Waubuno" and "Jane Miller" Disasters Recalled

◆

Another Georgian Bay Mystery

The search for the bodies of the ill-fated steamer J. H. Jones is being continued but up to the time of writing nothing has been discovered. . . . the chances are that the deep waters of the Georgian Bay will never give up the bodies of the Jones until the Judgement shall reveal the mystery of the wreck and the bodies of the dead shall be recalled and shall rehabilitate the souls of the lost passengers when the great trump shall sound and the bodies of the dead shall arise and meet at the Bar of God. So deep are the waters of the great Bay that only those who are lost in shallow water are ever recovered, as at the great depth the water is so cold that the little inland sea never gives up its dead.

Adapted from the Parry Sound North Star
December 5, 1906

PART TWO

*John Macaulay took charge of the search in the tense days after
the steamer Jones went missing.*

Chapter 9

ALL HANDS LOST

ON FRIDAY MORNING, the day after the *Jones* disappeared, the weather on Georgian Bay was clear and cold with bright skies. It was the sort of perfect fall day when it's easy to imagine that winter will never arrive.

In Lion's Head, the merchants grumbled that the *Jones* hadn't shown up on time. They needed their supplies. How were they supposed to run businesses when the boats were so unreliable? The local telegraph operator tried to reach Wiarton but no one answered at the

Crawford Tug offices, and there wasn't a single person in the town who knew the steamer's whereabouts. The rest of the peninsula's telegraph and telephone lines had all been grounded in Wednesday night's storm, so if the *Jones* had gone straight to Tobermory or tucked into some little cove to ride out the weather, there was no way to find out. The businessmen of Lion's Head would just have to wait.

By Friday afternoon, people in Wiarton and Lion's Head still hadn't heard anything from the *Jones* and it was beginning to get dark and blustery again. That night they went to bed in a storm and woke up to find their homes and streets covered in a white shroud. Then the weather got even worse.

With Jack Crawford out of town, tending to his mining interests, Dominion Fish Company manager John Macaulay, whose office was right beside the Crawfords', took charge. He told his men at the fish house that there was no cause for worry, that the *Jones* and her crew had been through worse storms than this. He went to speak to Lillie Crawford, to comfort and reassure her. He told her—as he did the other relatives of the *Jones*'s crew—that her husband was going to be fine, that all the old mariners were saying the *Jones* was probably in some little bay waiting it out. He mentioned that just that morning word had come from her own brother Will up in Barrow Bay, saying the *Jones*—or a boat that looked like her—had passed by the little village in the early hours. He told her that if there was no news by the next day, they'd begin a search by water.

Lillie and Jim's eldest son, fifteen-year-old Bert, had spent some time working on his father's boats by then and had friends down at the docks. He heard the stories that were going around, the rumours hanging in the air like languidly exhaled breaths of smoke, weaving in and out of streets and houses, clinging to the wallpaper, suffocating entire rooms. There was a man in Owen Sound telling anyone who'd listen that he'd planned to board the steamer but changed his mind at the last minute when he had a premonition of disaster. Several of the missing crew members had reportedly had foreboding hunches, telling their wives and families in Wiarton that they weren't sure about this last run of the year.

George Dobson, who was Macaulay's foreman at the fish house, had his own far-fetched tale. He told some of the other men that the captain's dog, Phelix, had also mysteriously disappeared the day the *Jones* left Owen Sound. Everyone in Wiarton knew the big dog; he was the size of a pony and had a loud, throaty bark. Captain Crawford had rescued him after a travelling theatre troupe performing *Uncle Tom's Cabin* (complete with live "bloodhounds" to track the runaway slaves) abandoned the sick creature. With the attention of the Crawfords, Phelix had recovered nicely. He became devoted to the captain and raced down to the dock whenever he heard the *Jones's* wildcat whistle. Just that summer Phelix had briefly gone missing and the captain had been so distraught he posted a notice in the *Echo* offering a reward for any information leading to his recovery.

According to Dobson, the day the *Jones* was last seen, Phelix showed up at the fish house around 4 p.m., though there had been no whistle to guide him to the harbour. He watched as the big dog ran out along the dock, then turned abruptly and broke into a gallop, heading northeast past the fish house and the cliffs lining the bay, lifting his head only to sniff the air. He hadn't seen the creature since, and felt quite certain the dog had died after jumping into the bay to rescue his master.

As the weekend dragged on and the storm raged, worry held Wiarton captive like an occupying army. There was no way to get away from it. Boats weren't running, the roads outside town were flooded and the regular stage-coach to Lion's Head and points north still wasn't in oper-ation. Mothers squeezed their children into woollen underwear and tried not to think about what was happen-ing on the open water. "God help the sailors on a night like this," they whispered as they passed one another on the darkened streets of town.

❦

Saturday, November 24, 1906, 7:30 a.m., Wiarton

John Macaulay hasn't slept well in days, what with the wind hammering the screen door at the back of the house (he has to get a new latch) and the spindly branches of the trees in the yard producing an eerie whistle as they lean toward the harbour. He's up anyway—even before the baby, who opens his eyes when the first blade of light enters his room—so he decides he might as well head down to the Dominion Fish offices on the waterfront.

It's faster to get to the fish house by wagon but Macaulay likes to walk sometimes. The dull creak of his feet on the wooden sidewalk is soothing to him, a kind of rhythmic white noise that allows his mind to wander. But today he can't find his pace and the wind is drowning out the sound of his steps. He pushes his hat down farther on his head and breathes in the cold air until his nostrils tingle. His nose feels like a block of ice, as if hit just the right way it would snap off and shatter onto the sidewalk.

Macaulay is getting more and more worried about the *Jones*. Word from Lion's Head is that she didn't call there yesterday afternoon, either. If she's holed up somewhere, or, worse, had engine or steering problems, the passengers will be panicking by now. Cold and wet and beaten. She's more than a full day late.

Macaulay sighs loudly and watches his frustration turn into clouds of moisture. He sighs again. Whenever anything goes wrong with a Wiarton boat, people expect him to sort it out. Margaret says he should be glad that people respect him so much. But he never asked for the responsibility. He has enough on his plate, thank you very much. And it's not exactly respect, anyway. It's just because they've all worked for him—in the fish house, at the fishing stations, on the docks or one of the boats—so they look to him when something's not right. It's not because they like him. There are people who grumble behind his back. The Indians at Cape Croker have been bad-mouthing him for years, saying he keeps them in debt for their equipment. He doesn't like it much when he hears they're telling people that you can go broke fishing for old Macaulay.

The door is locked when he tries to open the Crawford Tug Company office next to his own. Jack is still not back. Macaulay wired him the news about the *Jones* yesterday. He'll surely be home by tomorrow.

When he gets into his own office, Macaulay sits down at the desk, clears his throat and tries the telegraph office in Tobermory. The line is still grounded. He tries the telegraph lines to Providence Bay on Manitoulin and then Cockburn Island. All grounded. When he finally gets through to Meaford and Owen Sound, Penetang, Midland and Collingwood, there is no news at all.

Macaulay stands up to stretch his legs. Sending out other boats isn't possible—not yet, not with Colpoy's Bay still foaming and the wind blowing like a banshee from the northwest. He paces from his desk to the window and back again several times, then sits down.

Maybe Jim decided that it was safer to keep heading northwest into the wind rather than risk taking the waves on her beam. He'd be on Manitoulin by now. Macaulay taps the tip of his fountain pen against some papers. The more he thinks about the *Jones,* the more he's drawn back to Thursday morning. His memory of that day—the pungent smell of Owen Sound harbour, the frenzy of the crew rushing back and forth to the *Jones's* deck— becomes more and more exact. How heavy the boat looked plowing out of the harbour; how the crew lashed those coal-oil barrels together on their sides at the last minute. He wouldn't allow his men to do that. And certainly not so late in the fall when who knows what the bay would deliver. If the boat were to turn westward for Lion's Head, it would be struck on the side by big waves and the barrels might start rolling.

Macaulay rubs his eyes with the heel of his palms. He can hear the wind making a mournful song out of the shrouds attached to masts in the harbour. Snow flurries have transformed the rigging on the schooners into lacy ribbons.

He'll have to wait until there's word that someone has seen the boat. There's no use leaving the office to go into town with no news. He'll just have to face the mothers, daughters and wives of the crew and the captain. He'll have to tell them he has nothing for them. Nothing at all.

&&&

Sunday, November 25, 1906, 6 a.m., the Crawford house

Lillie stokes the kitchen stove and sits down at the table. The children are still asleep and the streets outside are deserted. Just the wind to keep her company. Like a living thing it's so noisy. She can almost convince herself it's a normal autumn Sunday. They'll have a big breakfast of eggs and sausage, griddle cakes and tea, then she'll bundle up the little ones and they'll all head off to the 8 a.m. church service together.

But there has been nothing about the last two days that is ordinary. When she went out to the dry-goods store yesterday the girl at the counter, who she's never said more than good day to, pressed her hand and whispered, "God bless" as she gave her her change. Lillie instinctively pulled her hand away. It embarrassed them both.

And the fiancée of one of Jim's crew—the Sadler boy, the second engineer—stopped her on the way home, right near the house, and embraced her. Imagine. The girl looked so desperate, her face pale and puffy— though she'd gone to the effort of putting rouge on her cheeks. When she tried to speak, her voice went up an octave and her breath got short. Eventually, she managed to choke out that they were to be married at Christmas, that just that week Wesley, her fiancé, had ordered a black four-button suit from Eaton's. Lillie had stepped back from her and nodded politely, her bad arm heavy as an anvil at her side.

Still, it wasn't the girls that upset her. It was John Macaulay, looking so hollow and wan, his usually immaculate suit crushed and tired. He's come by twice. He speaks in a matter-of-fact way, discounting the rumours that are passing through town. But everything about him—even his presence at the house—makes her wonder if his reassurances are meant as much for himself as for her.

Even little Eleanor and Dick seem to sense that something is not quite right. Eleanor has been clinging to her skirts, demanding to be held. And Dick has had two tantrums in two days. The older children have been trying to help out but yesterday afternoon she told them to leave, to go out and find their friends. She said that their father has been late before, God knows, and he'll surely be late again. All four of them, Madge, Whitney, Tyson and Bert, seemed glad to get away.

Lillie rakes her fingers through her loose hair and rubs her temples. She touches the papery skin beneath her eyes with the tip of her index finger. She feels old. Too old for the demands of small children. Too old for this kind of worry. Too old to care for this brood all on her own. Jim had better send word about where he is soon, she thinks fiercely, as if the force of her anger will ensure his survival.

She gets up and walks through the warm kitchen into the parlour. The familiar creak of the pine boards beneath her feet is more solace than any words John Macaulay can offer. The room is cold and slightly damp, but there's a view of the water from the front window. The bay is looking less ferocious this morning, the edges of the waves rounded like a dulled knife. Lillie shivers and grabs a throw blanket from the settee beneath the window. Awkwardly, she pulls it over her shoulders and adjusts it with her good arm. She can see the scrubby cedar trees near the Crawford sheds waving at her. Up above the branches, cracks in the white cliff leak water, like tears seeping from the rock.

⚜

Tuesday, November 27, 1906, noon, Wiarton

Fred Lyons is walking, calming his mind after taking the train from Owen Sound. He couldn't bear being alone there any longer. He needs to be close to other people who are waiting, as he is, for word of the *Jones*. He'll go down to the Crawford Tug Company offices once he looks into a few things himself.

The innkeeper at the Pacific told him that Mr. Flett at the Wiarton Carriage Works has a load on the boat and that he might have heard something. Fred has decided to stop by and inquire.

When he walks into Flett's dark warehouse crammed floor to crossbeam with carriages, democrats and sleighs, he notices several workmen huddled near the door. They look up at him when he enters, announced by a tinkle of bells on the door, but they don't know his face and ignore him.

The warehouse is enormous and Fred wanders around looking for Mr. Flett. But it doesn't look as if there is anyone here other than the men at the entrance. Heading back toward the door, he can hear the workmen still talking. "Isn't it *horrible?*" one of the men says, shaking his head. They pass their news one to the other like dogs sharing a bone.

"Two horse-drawn cutters from this shop," another says. "Some sailors' caps."

"The pilothouse was torn from the deck," one man offers.

Fred walks silently past the men and heads into the courtyard in front of the shop. His head feels like a drum stuffed with cloth to dull the sound. Maybe they were talking about something else. Another boat. He paces up and down in front of the carriage works, convincing himself that what he has just heard has nothing to do with him or the *J. H. Jones.* He passes the door twice. He doesn't dare go back in.

Fred tilts his hat so his eyes are shaded and straightens his back. He'll have to find John Macaulay. The rest of the farmers and fishermen in this godforsaken town are full of superstition, anyway. Untrustworthy. He heard a rumour going around Owen Sound that no one here wanted to start the search the day after the *Jones* left because it's bad luck to start a trip on a Friday. Macaulay wasn't very helpful when Fred inquired on the weekend, but he's no fool.

The snow of the last few days has melted, leaving the streets of Wiarton deep in mud. Striding down toward the water where the sidewalk ends, Fred's steps become slower and slower as the cinnamon sludge sucks at his boots. Occasionally he sinks so deep he has to grip the back of his knee to lift a leg. By the time he reaches the offices of the Dominion Fish Company he's so frustrated and tired he has to stop to catch his breath before he pushes the door open.

The room is in motion. A man is talking loudly into the telephone and there's another comforting a women who sobs on his shoulder. Her two children are standing beside her looking terrified, their backs straight as steel, eyes wide.

"The *Jones* is lost," Macaulay confirms when Fred approaches him. "We had word this morning that the Indians have found lifeboats and freight on Christian Island. Two boats are leaving here today to begin the search for survivors."

Trying to collect himself, Fred runs through scenarios in his mind. *Alex has survived.* If anyone could last in the water it's his brother. He's such a strong swimmer, a healthy young man. *His mother has survived.* She's cold and bewildered but alive. *He's giving the eulogy at their double funeral. He's comforting his sister. He's selling the family home.*

It takes every ounce of strength Fred has to tip his hat to Macaulay and ask that he be kept posted. He's about to leave the office when a man plows through the door, his feet hitting the wood like the slap of a beaver tail on water. He isn't large but he has a bigness about him. There are deep creases around his eyes and tiny red lines on his cheeks where it seems as if thousands of blood vessels have exploded. Macaulay's whole manner changes when he sees him. "Jack," he says.

The man leans his hands on his thighs to catch his breath. "Two bodies have been found at Big Bay," he blurts between gasps. "We must begin the search immediately."

Fred Lyons didn't plan on it but the first thing he does after trudging back into the main part of town is go to the telegraph office at the newspaper and wire his wife in Owen Sound. "The *Jones* is lost," he writes out, not trusting his voice. "Two bodies have been found but they have not been identified." He knows that by the time he gets home the news will have reached every corner of Owen Sound.

Fred returns to the hotel. The Pacific seemed serviceable enough when he checked in the day before, but now he notices the wallpaper is yellowed, the bedspread a threadbare strip of faded cotton. He wanders outside onto the second-floor porch. From there he can see the few remaining boats in the harbour rocking back and forth, the squeak of wooden bumpers against the dock muffled by the wind. Although it's prickly cold outside, it's a comfort to watch the sway of the tugs. Concentrating on the motion he finds his heart can return to its familiar rhythm. He thinks if he looks away even for a second it will start to beat like a hummingbird's wings.

Wednesday, November 28, 1906, 7 a.m., Christian Island

Jack Crawford is not a sailor. He's been around boats all his life, but it's Jim who got his captain's papers and Jim who knows about boat repairs and steam engines and flanges and fantails. The trip to Christian Island was mercifully calm, steaming out on the *Sanford* in tandem with the *Crawford*. People gathered at the town dock to send them off. Women waved sodden handkerchiefs, children huddled around their skirts. Jack wanted to shout to them with some brave sentiment but he couldn't think of anything to say.

The storm looked like it had subsided entirely when they reached the island. The shore was calm as they approached from the northwest, the trees appearing to rest after the violence of the previous week, wearily rustling when provoked by a breeze. But during the night the wind picked up again and the waves mounted, locking them at the dock of the Indian village on the south shore.

Now Jack is trying to act as if he isn't feeling sick, as if his stomach isn't performing acrobatics each time he loses sight of the horizon. Rutherford, the captain of the *Sanford*, has the good grace to ignore his lurching to the rail, but he knows some members of the crew have been snickering behind their hands at him. He's nobody's fool. He'll make sure they don't work on his boats again.

It's being trapped, Jack thinks, that makes him feel so seasick. That and the task before them. He's begun to calculate the damage a wreck means to the company. She's valued at $12,000 but with no marine insurance this time of year, they'll have to absorb the loss. It's not that he's cold-hearted, doing arithmetic at a time like this. His own flesh and blood is on board, and he knows every one of the other men personally. But he has to be practical. And it won't do any good to be melancholy now when there's still an outside chance there are survivors. Anyway, if Crawford Tug is ruined, it will affect more than just his own pocketbook.

Jack and Macaulay gather on the *Sanford's* deck to discuss plans for the day. Sipping dark, hot tea, they agree that their priority should be to look for people who are alive. They've both heard of stranger things. Someone could be lying unconscious on the island or a nearby shore.

But there's no use going out on the rough water today, risking more lives; they'll have to begin on land.

The crew disembarks and climbs onto the wagons they will take to the western beach where wreckage has been found. Jack instructs the men to watch particularly for bodies, even pieces of clothing. It is imperative that anything connected to the passengers and crew be handled with utmost care. Only debris from the boat has been discovered so far. The two bodies found near Big Bay turned out to be unlucky local fishermen caught in the same storm as the *Jones*.

A small group of islanders led by the Indian chief Montague and Reverend Wilson, the Methodist missionary, take Jack and Macaulay and the others along deeply rutted roads to the shore. When they arrive, Jack immediately spots two of the *Jones's* lifeboats stowed away from the beach in the shelter of some cedar trees. One of the yawls is in perfect condition with the oars still intact. The men used it, the missionary explains, to reach the broken fragments of the wheelhouse, which someone spotted floating out past the shore on Saturday morning. The rescuers nearly drowned trying to drag the unwieldy object to land. The wheelhouse's two narrow windows are shattered, shards of glass like sharpened teeth stuck in the frame.

While Jack is inspecting the splintered wood, an Indian woman approaches him. She says something in Ojibway that Jack doesn't understand and places a small object in his hand. He recognizes it right away. It's a stamp with a small wooden handle and a piece of flesh-coloured rubber at the end carved with the words *Crawford Tug Company Ltd*. It lies in his palm like a feather.

✺

Thursday, November 29, 1906, 5 p.m., Christian Island

There's an odd kind of stillness on the water after a storm. It's almost as if the two-storey waves never happened, as if the wind didn't beat the trees horizontal, the force of the water didn't crush giant slabs of rock into pebbles. The bay seems to taunt you in those placid post-storm moments—denying all knowledge of its cruel and ugly side, as if you're the one that's crazy.

John Macaulay knows he isn't crazy, but he is shaken. The tension when the *Jones* didn't call at her destinations, the women with their tears, the joking bravado of the men that turned suddenly into grave, told-you-so sternness when they heard the news of the wreckage. He is tired and sorry and shocked into dullness.

Isaac Lennox and Dr. McEwan, the fathers of two of the *Jones*'s crew members, arrived on the *Waubaushene* this morning. Macaulay knows that they hope that if anyone comes across the bodies of their sons they will be there to wrap them in linen and touch their cold hands. It's difficult to watch them finger the life preservers, look searchingly at the caps that have been found, as if they might recognize their boys in the stitching. They haven't broken down yet, but their forebearance, the quiet earnestness they both maintain, is hard to watch.

It was particularly horrible that morning when a photograph of Ed Lennox washed up on the west beach. Macaulay could hardly look Isaac in the face. He just kept thinking about how he'd spoken to young Ed before the

Jones sailed. The first mate had been deferential, stooping slightly as he always did to not seem quite so tall and gangly, tucking his arms behind his back.

Macaulay wants to tell Isaac this. He wants to press his hand and say what a good man his son was. He wants to tell him how impressed everyone in town was when Ed was made first mate at such a young age, when so many older fellows with more experience were passed by. But he doesn't because when he has a chance, when they're together searching the island for the debris that is still washing up in dribs and drabs, he can't even choke out a syllable.

And then, when he is finally able to clear his throat enough to talk, he sputters out something that he regrets immediately. Something about the Indians making like the busy bee to lay their honey by, hiding Mr. Flett's sleighs beneath the cedar trees near the beach. Lennox squints at him and McEwan says (rather sharply, Macaulay thinks), "Who knows that some whites wouldn't do the same?" It is awkward and Macaulay resolves to be quiet.

Now the light is almost gone, the search over for the day. The smell of cedar smoke is intense on shore when Macaulay and the others spot a trio of tugs headed toward the island. The boats look tired, lazily displacing white lips of water as they plow forwards and backwards looking for a place to tie up. One of the search boats has already set off for the mainland but several other vessels are planning to stay at least another night to continue looking for bodies. No one has much hope left of finding anyone alive. Not after a full week.

After supper, the men gather on the *Sanford* to take stock. No one has much more to report. They're weak from fatigue and frustrated. The shoreline is sandy in some places but rocky in most and the small stones are striped black and white, others shot through with pink quartz or flecks of silver. Their many shapes and hues make it difficult to see anything among them. And the island is big, the west coast where most of the debris has been found a wild stretch of unpopulated surf and stone.

The crew of one of the tugs found some hay, a case of apples and bags of flour that were sopping wet on the outside but sprayed the men with fluffy white powder when they slashed them open. There were also some shipping papers scattered on the shore, and someone discovered a club bag belonging to Jim Donaldson of the Wolverine Fish Company. He would have had money in it to pay the fishermen, but there's nothing left inside.

To a man, the searchers are pale, their eyes rimmed with red. Today, Macaulay overheard two of the sailors talking fiercely about how someone has to take responsibility for the disaster. How their comrades were sacrificed to the storm, to business. Other men joined in. Tension is still thick tonight and Macaulay worries there might be a fight. But after they discuss the day's search, the sailors sleepwalk to their berths in the forecastle, too tired to argue.

Their sullen faces and few harsh words are enough to persuade Macaulay that he is right to keep to himself a small clock he found tucked behind a piece of wood on the beach. There's something about it that makes everything seem too final. The sailors and other members of the search party need to keep their hopes up for now.

Macaulay picks up the little clock and rolls it over in his hand. The metal around the face is dented and the glass is bubbled with moisture but he'd recognize it anywhere. Ten years ago he himself mounted it in the wheelhouse of the *J. H. Jones.* The hands are stopped at 4:15.

It was agony, the waiting, the lack of resolution. For Lillie and the other wives who had only absence to mark their loss; for the small children who believed their fathers would still come bursting in the door, all red cheeks and whiskers.

Chapter 10

THE SADDEST CALAMITY

THE LAST OF THE *Jones* search party returned to
Wiarton two weeks after the boat disappeared. They had
little to offer the town's six widows and their sixteen children, or the others in Wiarton and elsewhere who'd lost
friends and relatives.

Businessmen had formed the Steamer *Jones* Disaster
Fund to help the Wiarton families through Christmas.
The merchants rallied the townspeople, soliciting produce
from farmers and money from whomever could spare it.

The county council donated $200. But things were tight. There were never enough jobs in the wintertime and the economy had been on a slide since the sugar beet factory failed. People dug in their pockets for coins and hoped the winter would be a short one.

In the harbour beneath the white cliffs and on the red-brick buildings in town flags flew at half-mast. Stores on Berford Street covered their windows in black paper. A memorial service was arranged for the middle of December.

On the day of the service, members of the local fraternal societies gathered at the town hall to wind their way through the streets to the Methodist Church. They brought their banners but walked in silence, the crunch of frozen mud and snow underfoot a kind of rhythmic homage to the dead. Ministers from four of the town's churches shared the pulpit that day, advising the community to pray for the families of the crew and passengers. Women dressed in black sobbed and hugged their children. The Christmas oranges that had started to arrive at stores on Berford Street did nothing to lift the gloom.

But the wreck brought more than grief to the little town. It brought notoriety, and it wasn't the kind of national attention Wiarton's early boosters had once imagined. The *Jones* was big news—making the front page of all the Toronto newspapers. There were still editors and reporters who remembered the selling potential of the *Asia* tragedy.

"STEAMER JONES GOES DOWN WITH OVER TWENTY SOULS," blasted *The Globe*. A small boxed-off section promised "The Mute Story of Disaster." Files were dredged up about the wrecks of the *Waubuno* and the *Jane*

Miller; readers were reminded darkly that both had happened on the same late-November date, twenty-seven and twenty-nine years before *to the day.*

Not to be outdone, the Toronto *News* started a collection for the family of a passenger named Daniel McIvor. Merchants in the village of Providence Bay on Manitoulin Island had written a letter to the newspaper, asking if the editors might publicize the case of Mrs. McIvor who was widowed by the disaster, left with six children under the age of eleven to support on her own. The tiny village, the businessmen explained, was already struggling from a poor harvest when the *Jones* went down, taking both McIvor and a prominent merchant named Thomas Wagg with it. The loss was enormous. The McIvor Fund, as it became known, received an unprecedented response. Bible classes and other sympathetic readers donated nearly $500 to the destitute family.

No one could say exactly how many other passengers were on the *Jones*. The only record was lost with the steamer. People who'd seen the boat loading talked about seeing a mother and father with their three children, and young men going to work the timber limits at Silverwater on Manitoulin Island, but nobody knew their names. The number of people lost vacillated between twenty and thirty. For a time it seemed as if every missing person in the country had been on the boat. The wife of a Rochester lumberman named Ambrose Majeau claimed that her husband must have been a passenger since he hadn't written home in weeks. But by the middle of December Mr. Majeau was discovered keeping residence in a Collingwood hotel. The official count was more or less established at eighteen passengers and twelve crew. In the weeks of searching before the ice came in, not one of the victims of the *Jones* was found.

It was agony, the waiting, the lack of resolution. For the wives who had only absence to mark their loss; for the small children who believed their fathers would still come bursting in the door, all red cheeks and whiskers. The suddenness of their deaths, the awful mystery about what happens to a body lost at sea made it especially hard to bear. As winter buffeted the Bruce Peninsula, the families of the *Jones*'s passengers and crew began to realize that victims of the wreck might never be found.

Then, just before the ice came in, bubbles of oil were discovered three miles from Cape Croker, marking—some people believed—where the steamer had foundered. There was talk about a renewed search in that location, but nothing could be done until after the spring thaw. The *Toronto Daily Star* reminded its readers ominously that "The deep waters of Georgian Bay never give up their dead." Without bodies to wash and dress and mourn, there could be no burials, no proper funerals. No end.

The town entered a state of suspended animation. Some of the lost sailors were members of fraternal orders that paid out life insurance. Thank-you notices from wives and mothers who'd been sent cheques appeared in the *Echo*. But many other families had no insurance, no savings or means of support once the relief fund ran out. The wife and five children of deckhand James Tilley depended on the goodwill of Wiarton Town Council to supply their home with water. Lillie Crawford and the children were lucky to have the Tyson family and Jack Crawford to help them out or they, too, would have been destitute that winter.

The cause of the wreck remained the subject of intense speculation on the streets of Wiarton. People tried on theories like new hats. The boiler exploded. The steering failed. The oil barrels smashed through the gangway doors. The waves bashed the little steamer to pieces. The passengers and crew were trapped like rats in a cage. The captain was drunk. The steamer was overloaded. Too small. Too old. Too slow.

The *Echo* had proclaimed it "the saddest calamity that has ever befallen Wiarton," saying, "How the accident occurred is a mere matter of conjecture. . . ." But, perhaps mindful of the fact that other newspapers would take its lead, several paragraphs later, the *Echo* described the captain and crew as "old mariners, thoroughly competent," adding the more pointed disclaimer, "The wreck was not due to any want of competency upon the part of any of those on board."

It didn't stop the rumours. It didn't stop the *Owen Sound Sun* from publishing a letter to the editor suggesting that "a painful impression is gaining general ground around town" that the *Jones* had been overloaded, that the owners were greedy, that the captain had bad judgment going out in a little boat that couldn't handle the fall gales. The *Parry Sound North Star* on the other side of the bay claimed "there was only one safe thing for the captain of the *Jones* to do and that was to lie safe in the harbor of Owen Sound until the gale . . . had blown over. . . . Captain Crawford pulled out . . . in a small steamer with a big load of freight, badly loaded and stowed . . . and risked the lives of himself and his helpless passengers and crew."

As time passed, the differing views about what had happened to the *Jones* formed into factions. Middleton

Crawford told the family's version to a newspaperman from the Toronto *News*. He explained that the steamer was likely wrecked by waves beating against her broadside when she turned at Cape Croker toward Lion's Head. With a heavy load of cargo she wouldn't have been able to recover from the force of the waves.

But it was John Macaulay's growing conviction about the role of the improperly loaded coal-oil barrels that hardened into fact in many Wiarton homes. Though there was some dispute about the number—Macaulay said twenty-five, while others claimed as few as seven barrels had been rolled onto the boat—most sailors on the Bruce agreed that big waves alone could not have toppled the staunch steamer *Jones*. The storm had definitely been bad, but as Macaulay later explained to a newspaper reporter, if the barrels hadn't been bashing back and forth "perhaps one or two to begin with and then the others adding and piling up their weight," the boat would have made it to Lion's Head.

In the weeks and years that followed, Wiarton's newspaper was cautious not to assign blame or champion any view about the cause of the disaster. Maybe the editors felt the need to protect the families of the dead from accusations. The fact that by the early 1900s, the Crawford and Tyson families were related to a large number of people in town through marriage or birth—including an uncle who was a newspaper editor—might also have helped. Or perhaps they were simply being circumspect, given the lack of facts. But, as my grandmother Eleanor would later understand as clearly as a brand on her forehead, there were many people in Wiarton who believed that her father, Captain Crawford—ultimately responsible for the badly loaded

coal-oil barrels and for leaving Owen Sound in a storm—
was to blame.

From the beginning there had been rumours that the
captain was spotted in an Owen Sound hotel just before
leaving port. He'd thrown back his head to drink a shot of
whisky and announce, "Bah! We've been through worse
storms than this!" As public opinion began to harden on the
captain's role in the disaster—as families began to feel the
effect of a winter with no paycheque, as weeks passed with
no more news of debris or bodies—people also remembered other stories about Jim Crawford. Crew members
recounted near misses on his steamers; they recalled the
suspicious drowning of Harry Varco, the steward from
the *Joe Milton;* some said they had always suspected he was
a drinker and womanizer. Jim Crawford's admired tenacity
became stubbornness, his sailor's courage flagrant risk taking with the lives of others—perhaps even murder.

That winter, empty factory buildings on the edge of
Colpoy's Bay taunted people with their promise. Houses
lay vacant; more farms were abandoned. "The 20th century
belongs to Canada," the newspaper reminded the people of
Wiarton, recalling Prime Minister Sir Wilfrid Laurier's
famous phrase. But it always felt hollow, even threatening,
as if the Canada Laurier was talking about was not the old
country of Confederation, not the former frontier lands of
Ontario. The Canada he spoke of had moved west and
north, south to the industrialized cities, leaving ghost
towns in its wake, villages populated by old people and
overgrown farms. In the still, low light of winter it became
harder and harder to remember which came first—the
wreck of the *Jones* or the wreck of the town.

Many of Wiarton's young men had already headed to Cobalt, in the north, where a blacksmith had thrown his hammer at a fox and hit a rich vein of silver instead. To Alberta and Saskatchewan, newly minted provinces carved out of the old boundaries of the Northwest Territories. To Winnipeg, where Eaton's had opened a shimmering new department store, complete with a fine dining establishment, attendants in the washroom and a sea of crisp merchandise.

Fifteen-year-old Bert was the first of the Crawford children to leave town. He was still a boy, but after his father's death he was told he would have to be the man of the family. He'd always been a happy-go-lucky child, a pack of friends by his side, hunting and fishing with his grandpa Tyson. He'd worked on the boats, hauling fish from the stations down to the plant in Wiarton, but now Lillie begged him not to go on the bay. What really interested him, anyway, was automobiles. By the end of December, he'd found an apprenticeship in Brantford at the locomotive works. He told his friends and family he thought he'd work for Henry Ford himself one day. He sent home what he could spare after paying for food and rent.

Tyson was next. He was thirteen and intellectually precocious, a member of the high school Shakespearean society. Lillie arranged for him to stay with her younger brother and his wife in Manitoba. They were childless then. Lillie knew it was the only way the boy would ever get an education.

He left a little more than a month after his father's death, taking the train westward, tracing the edge of Lake Superior, on to a little village called Holland on a twisty stretch of the Assiniboine River in Manitoba. Lillie's brother had moved there soon after he graduated from the pharmacy program at the University of Toronto. He'd married a girl named Clara Belle Beach. Tyson became like a son to the two of them, insulated from his father's shame, from the tragedy of the *Jones*.

❧

January 8, 1907, Wiarton

It's a relief that the children are out of the house. The two boys are coasting on Greenlees hill; Madge is with little Eleanor, who still walks headlong, like a runaway wagon. She needs to be watched constantly. Lillie warned Madge that with the older boys gone she'll have to watch out for the young ones and not get into any scrapes.

Lillie closes her eyes and leans back in her rocking chair. She can feel the bones in her shoulders against the carved wood. Someone in town will be sure to report that her children are behaving like savages. She doesn't care. Not today. Not right now. They've been cooped up together for too long. She needs some time by herself. Time to think.

It's been six weeks since the *Jones* disappeared. At first when she realized that the steamer was definitely lost, she fainted. People had thought she'd had another stroke. All the strength she had imagined she possessed seemed to melt into a puddle at her feet. Now, most of the time, she doesn't feel anything at all.

It was a few days before her father finally told her what people were saying about Jim, about how the wreck was his fault. He advised her to keep the children out of school until the talk blew over. Their presence would only feed the rumours, he said. But her father was wrong. The stories persisted despite their silence. Lillie tried to shield the children against it, but Whitney had come home just the other day, his shirt in tatters. He had his head down when he pushed through the kitchen door. He didn't look at her, didn't even say hello, just skulked upstairs to the room he shared with Dick. Lillie made Madge tell her what happened in the schoolyard. She said Whitney had the tar beaten out of him after he'd swung at someone who'd called their father names.

Lillie misses the older boys. It was difficult to say goodbye. But it was the right thing—for their own sakes. Bert will be fine, he's just that sort of boy. But Tyson is so sensitive. A letter came from him yesterday. He told her all about the train trip out there and about the big house where they live. How his uncle got fed up with Clara always out playing the organ for the church choir and tied her to the pump in the backyard! He said to say hello to the others. He seems happy, though he asked in the postscript when he'd be coming home.

Lillie gets up to put the kettle on for some tea and sits back down again. She gets tired so easily these days. She doesn't even have the energy to read most of the time. All she can think about is how they will make ends meet this year. Her family helped tide them over the last while but she'll have to come up with something else soon. Jack says there won't be much for anyone from the sale of Crawford Tug.

She hadn't wanted to take anything from the disaster relief fund, not with others suffering so much more. But they'll soon need something. Madge is growing and will have to have new clothes this spring. The others can make do with hand-me-downs but there are also medical bills and repairs to the house and the wagon. She gave away Phelix—though the children weren't happy about it. Her father said people in town think he drowned out by Cape Croker. But she just couldn't afford to keep him. His droopy eyes and disappointment each time the door opened were too much to bear.

Lillie's father has advised her to sell the house. But she can't bring herself to contemplate leaving behind the garden she dug with her own hands, the rooms she carefully wallpapered with Jim when they were first married.

It is her anger that still surprises her. She imagines it as a small black tumour at the base of her throat—sometimes it just sits there, benign, other times it grows, spreading like a cancer, choking her.

The other day her sister Susie set her off. She brought God into it, said all that had happened was His will. A test of Faith. That it must be for the Best. Lillie snapped. Pointing to the children playing on the floor, she asked angrily if leaving those babies without a father was part of some grand plan? If all the suffering in town was "meant to be"? Lillie had rarely seen her unflappable younger sister get roused, but Susie's ears flamed and blotchy marks appeared on her neck. She left the house without saying a word, letting the screen door slam on her way out.

After the service on Sunday morning Mother had insisted they speak to one another. They talked quietly, about the sermon and the cost of milk, dancing around the subject of their disagreement.

When they parted, Susie had smiled at her, a flicker of pity animating her eyes. Lillie felt her stomach lurch like a sailboat in a sudden gust. She resolved not to say another word to her sister about how she felt. It took all her willpower to smile back and nod goodbye, her mouth dry, her throat constricted.

꿍

It was the middle of January 1907—the crepe paper recently removed from store windows in Wiarton, flags tugged back to the top of flagpoles—when a Native boy made a grisly discovery about three miles northwest of the Christian Island lighthouse. The beach is sandy there, big white dunes blown up from the water's edge, low-lying cedar trees and twisted white pine growing a safe distance from the crashing waves. It's almost always windy, barren and deserted in the winter.

The boy was out for a walk—hoping perhaps to find more evidence of the shipwreck, or looking to escape from winter in the close little village—when he came across a body of a young man dressed in a dark serge suit and lace-up boots, a life preserver stencilled with the words *J. H. Jones* tied around his waist. The body was partly caught in the ice and the boy struggled to drag the heavy bloated corpse onto shore. He was sweating when he finally managed to get it clear of the water's frozen grip and turn it over. He sat beside the body to catch his breath and saw for the first time that the young man's face was gone, from his chin to the back of his head, worn off by rocks and ice.

When Jack Crawford heard the news he left Wiarton immediately and headed to Penetang where the corpse had been transported. Fred Lyons caught another train from Owen Sound, convinced it was his brother, Alex.

At the undertaker's, the man's jacket pockets were emptied and the items carefully noted: a gold fob watch, $1.25 in silver and five cents in coppers, a jackknife, a handkerchief, an aluminum comb and a small Webster's dictionary.

The dead man was young, with reddish hair, but it wasn't Alexander Lyons. The contents of the man's pockets were carefully repeated in newspaper accounts so that his family might recognize him by his belongings. It took several weeks before two brothers came forward to claim the body of Richard Addison.

People in Wiarton prepared themselves to hear about more bodies. In May when the ice pushed another corpse up on White Cloud Island at the mouth of Colpoy's Bay, Jack Crawford rushed to the scene again. But this time it wasn't a victim of the *Jones*, but a man from Cape Croker who'd drowned with four others soon after the *Jones* went down. It was the final straw for Jack. He was frayed and tired. In desperation he offered a cash reward for recovery of the bodies of Jim Crawford, engineer Charles Shaw and two other crew members. Quietly, he tried to sell the Crawford Tug Company. The new Wiarton concern, Peninsula Tug & Towing, was a possible buyer. Will Tyson, Lillie's brother and a former Crawford Tug Company master, said he'd like to buy the *Crawford*.

By the summer, Jack had decided that continuing the search was fruitless. Isaac Lennox and Dr. McEwan went to Christian Island twice in July and August, combing the rocks and water for evidence of the *Jones*. And some of the other families hired a man who spent a week dragging an anchor along the bottom near Cape Croker. Nothing was found.

In August 1907, the two waterlogged and battered wooden cutters that had been stowed on the *Jones* were returned to Wiarton carriage maker James Flett. He wondered loudly if they were even worth the $16 the Christian Island Indians charged him for transporting them back to the mainland. He placed one outside his shop. A souvenir. People stood around the sleigh, running their hands over the splintered wood, trying to imagine its terrible voyage.

*On one side of my family, Georgian Bay meant work and sacrifice;
on the other it was lazy days spent swimming and fishing.*

Chapter 11

The Summer People

WIARTON HAS NEVER amounted to much. Not, at least, compared to the dreams of the early town fathers. It never became *the* City of the North. It never even became a city. It simply couldn't recover from the advent of the twentieth century. In the thirty years after the wreck of the *Jones*, the collapse of the lumber industry and then the slow, demolition of the fishery (through overfishing and the accidental introduction of the predatory lamprey eel into the Great Lakes) sounded the death knell for the town's prosperity.

Today, the harbour is busy in summer with daytripping sailors and powerboaters stopping for fuel and supplies, but there's an abandoned feeling about the town itself. It is especially so in winter when streets and faces are grey, the trees bare. Bargain shops line the lone main street, and many of the grand old houses up on the hill are rented out as apartments or Victorian-style bed and breakfasts. The mill that's still standing has become a family-style restaurant.

The town's main claim to fame these days is as the home of Wiarton Willie, a small albino groundhog, who is known by his promoters as Canada's "leading weather prognosticator." Like Punxsutawney Phil, Shubenacadie Sam and their hapless brethren, Willie's job is to poke his head out of a hole on February 2—Groundhog Day— when the sight of his shadow is thought to predict the imminent end of winter. Organizers estimate that tens of thousands of people pay homage to the "hog" each year during the week-long festival that includes a Wake-up Willie party and the annual "Magic of Willie" parade.

Despite the success of this event and the natural beauty of its location, Wiarton remains the sort of town that young people leave. There simply aren't enough jobs or much else to keep them. There are fewer people living there today than when my grandmother Eleanor was a child.

But in those days, enterprising citizens still hadn't lost hope in their ability to recapture the prosperity of an earlier era. When my grandmother was young, people in Wiarton spent a great deal of time trying to figure out what had gone wrong in the once-bustling town. The newspaper spearheaded a fault-finding campaign. Local council was blamed. People who bought mail order from

Eaton's were blamed. Schools that neglected to teach agriculture in favour of Shakespeare and Milton were accused of causing Wiarton's decline. Big cities were the problem. Wages were too low. Taxes too high. There was no spirit in the place, editorialists complained. What Wiarton obviously needed, the newspaper said, wagging an accusatory finger, was a Booster Club, like the sort other towns had formed to promote their interests to industry and small business.

But nothing seemed to work for very long. There weren't many industries willing to locate in a dying town. The coasting boats stopped regular service as cars and more extensive rail lines replaced them. Property values dropped even further as people moved away. A teenage Eleanor complained bitterly that there was nothing doing in Wiarton. She longed to escape.

Many of the town's citizens trumpeted tourism as the saviour for their flagging fortunes. Public meetings were held to discuss how to make Wiarton more appealing to visitors; the *Echo* published whole issues devoted to the attractions of the town and the region. The ladies of the Women's Institute spent weeks cleaning and clearing the waterfront. Enlisting the assistance of several men and a team of horses, they cleansed the beach of its sawmill past, erecting fireplaces and small cottages that were available to let.

Wiarton wasn't alone in its attempts to come to terms with a new economy; in the early decades of the century the rest of the Georgian Bay region was also experiencing a move away from resource exploitation. Settlers and land speculators were headed farther north and west into unexplored territories where land was cheap and rich with minerals and trees. For many Georgian Bay towns and villages, tourism began to seem like a perfect solution. People living on the bay would still be dependent on summer traffic, but traffic of a different sort.

Jonathan and Elizabeth Dowler, my great-grandparents on my father's side, arrived on Georgian Bay in the summer of 1914. The Canadian Pacific Railway branch line tracing the eastern side of the water was finished then, although many of the summer people still travelled the shore by passenger steamer. Several beautiful and rugged hotels had been built onto the rock at Pointe au Baril and elsewhere to serve tourists looking to fish or take the fresh-air cure.

The Dowlers hailed from southwestern Ontario, Irish haberdashers with a thriving storefront trade in London and St. Thomas. They'd heard about Pointe au Baril from Jonathan's brother, R.H., who'd explored the area in the years before the railway arrived. R.H. liked to tell a story about his first trip there, when he took a steamer from Penetang, then hired a guide and rowboat to take him from the dock in Pointe au Baril out to the pretty, new cedar-shake Ojibway Hotel. It was a bit of a journey in a little boat and they had to row hard, weaving in and out of rocks and islands. R.H. was enormously relieved when they came around a corner and saw the three-storey hotel with its wide front porch rising out of the rocks like a sentinel of civility in the middle of the forest. They pulled up to the docks, exhausted and hungry at 6:05 p.m., only to have the proper-looking owner inform them that he was dreadfully sorry he couldn't help them, dinner was over. The dining room had closed at six o'clock.

R. H. Dowler, however, was not the sort to hold a grudge. Over the years he returned regularly to the Ojibway, even spending his honeymoon at the hotel.

My paternal great-grandparents and their children spent their first summer at Pointe au Baril camped on a rocky point about ten miles south of the railway station, while Jonathan looked for land to build a cottage. Eventually he persuaded a squatter named Tom Smith— known locally for his near-encyclopedic knowledge of the waters—to sell twenty-eight acres with a sandy beach near the Shawanaga Indian Reserve. When the family decided to build a cottage there three years later, the timber, paint and even nails were brought up on a flatcar from St. Thomas.

While the cottage was being built in the summer of 1917, the Dowler family lived in a giant canvas house tent with four bedrooms and a dining room. The cookhouse, where Elizabeth and the maid prepared fresh pickerel and smallmouth bass for family and guests, was set up out back.

My grandmother Pat was the Dowler's second child, a toddler when they first arrived in Pointe au Baril, and she loved to tell stories about those early days. She made it sound romantic, describing her father and mother as brave pioneers. Her arms would fly in the air, eyes alight, her voice trilling out certain words for effect. She had an infectious, cackling laugh that nearly drowned her words in its giddy burbling. She would sit at the big pine table in the cottage kitchen or in a bouncing metal chair in the screened-in porch and regale us with familiar stories, completely unconcerned that she had told the same one the day or week before. We would all beg her to recount our favourites. I loved to hear the one about the sulky

August days when she and her siblings and cousins would go searching in bogs and swamps for giant bullrushes that had dried on the stalk. Then, late at night, out in an old red rowboat, they would douse them in kerosene, flames lighting the bay on fire.

When I was little, we called my grandmother Tugboat Nanny. She encouraged it, wearing the skipper's hats we bought her and squeezing enthusiastically on the handheld horn placed near the wheel of her pale blue and white tugboat.

In the mid 1960s, she and my grandfather had gone to considerable lengths to find this boat. They'd just built their own place on a small island within sight of the mainland and the old Dowler family cottage (sold by then to family friends), and they wanted a distinctive vessel. They spent months one fall scouring the north shore of Lake Erie, stopping when they found the perfect yawl in a junkyard in Port Colbourne. It had been a lifeboat on an old freighter but the ship was being dismantled and the parts sold. They put down $500, had it stripped of decades of old paint, added a wheelhouse and a reconditioned motor. They called it a tug and named it *Waukon II* after a steamer called the *Waukon* that had delivered groceries, mail, telegrams and cottagers when my grandmother was a child. Long and narrow and pointed at both bow and stern, the *Waukon II* rolled in the waves like a metronome set for waltz time. It was similar to the metal lifeboat that saved the lives of the *Asia* survivors, Christy Ann Morrison and Duncan Tinkiss—a boat that also ended up spending its dotage in Pointe au Baril, reconditioned as a fishing vessel and used for forays up the shore.

My grandfather passed away not long after they bought the *Waukon II*, but Tugboat Nanny carried on, becoming a celebrated sight in the area as she manoeuvred her slow, awkward old craft spilling over with wicker picnic baskets, grandchildren and her grey-haired friends. I remember many long, lazy trips dodging the islands and shoals. My brother and I liked to chase one another around the perimeter of the tug, then sit in the stern over the vibrating motor, shaken into silence, trailing our hands in the cold splash off the sides.

Tugboat Nanny died a few months before the planned celebrations to mark her eightieth year at Pointe au Baril. But the cottage she and my grandfather built is a place that still creaks and snaps with her presence. There are many things that haven't been moved in the decade since she spent her last summer there. A chunk of pink quartz sits on the mantel of the big stone fireplace. A wooden yoke once used to carry water is hung over a window. And near the fireplace, tucked behind a bucket full of wood, there is a big block of coal rescued from The Wreck.

I was only a few weeks old when my parents carried me up to Pointe au Baril for the first time. It's where I learned to sail and swim, how to catch minnows and net a fish. I baked my skin on its rocks and screamed my fifteen-year-old angst into the wind. It is there, under a big dome of sky that I found the space to imagine my life.

I've thought often about how it is that while I run *to* Georgian Bay, my grandmother Eleanor ran away. I associate the bay with lazy days spent swimming and reading and applying sunscreen; for her and the Crawford side of my family, Georgian Bay was work and sacrifice. It was fishing boats and rolling log booms, coal oil and black smoke fouling the air. It was dirt and loss and death.

All her life my grandmother Eleanor considered Wiarton, particularly, and the Georgian Bay region in general, a sooty, claustrophobic place. When I was a baby and my parents were considering moving to the town, not far from the bay, where I would grow up, Eleanor begged them to reconsider. It's Ontario's Bible Belt, she told them with a raise of her eyebrows. It's narrow-minded and depressed, she warned. But they moved there anyway because they liked the town and my father found a good job. I don't think she ever stopped wondering how they ever could have *chosen* such a home.

*I hoped that if I looked at the pictures in her locket closely
enough, I could make sense of my grandmother's life.*

Chapter 12

THE LOCKET

WHEN MY GRANDMOTHER was a girl, she was given a gold locket by her mother. After she died, it was passed on to me. Oval and slightly larger than a quarter, it's perfect for rubbing between thumb and forefinger. Something about its smooth polished surface and the way it's worn down in the middle makes me think my grandmother thought so too.

Inside, there are two photographs facing one another. On the right is a picture of her brother Tyson taken during the First World War. He's dressed in his Highlander battalion's uniform—a woollen jacket with brass buttons at the collar and a glengarry that slopes precisely across his forehead. He's got the kind of narrow moustache that would be relegated to the trash bin of infamy by the end of the Second World War. If the picture hadn't been cut to fit the tiny frame, you'd also see his kilt, knee socks and white spats. Looking at him you can't help thinking that he is standing especially erect, hands clasped behind his back, eyes averted, gazing into the distance. He wears the weight of his responsibility like a medal pinned to his chest.

Opposite Tyson is the photo of a young girl, a giant bow at the back of her hair. She's squinting into the sun but even so you can see she has the sharp glint of mischief in her eyes. The faint outline of a farmhouse can be seen in the distance. It's Helen Murphy, Eleanor's best friend.

I've looked at these pictures often, opening and closing the slightly tarnished locket with a satisfying click, wondering what they meant to Eleanor. What they helped her to remember. Where these two people fit into the story she told about herself. I imagined her choosing these pictures carefully. I hoped that if I looked at them closely enough I could make some more sense of her life, of what she gave up when she left her past behind.

I knew from my mother that Tyson was Eleanor's favourite brother. He'd lived with his uncle from the time he was thirteen until he joined the army nine years later. He'd studied pharmacy at the University of Manitoba. But he would come home each summer for a few weeks to see his mother and siblings. He was kind to Eleanor then—which is more than she could say about some of her other brothers.

When the photo in the locket was taken, Tyson was in Wiarton for a few days before his Vancouver-based battalion left for England and the battlefields of Europe. It was April 20, 1916, three weeks after his twenty-third birthday, a week before Eleanor's eleventh. A battalion from the Bruce Peninsula was getting organized when he arrived. Churches were vying for the recruits' attendance; banquets and concerts and dances were held. Someone even sent the men fifty boxes of homemade candy and offered to provide them with cigars whenever they liked. It was only beginning to dawn on Canadians that they were sending their young men off to slaughter.

Eleanor was mesmerized by her brother in his 72nd Seaforth Highlander's uniform. In her scrapbooks and the boxes of photographs she kept for the rest of her life there are numerous images taken in those short spring days before Tyson left for war. In each photo he's dressed in full regalia, holding a small baton in his hand. It gives him an air of authority—like a bandleader.

Tyson was a small man but dashing in uniform, with slicked-back hair, deep-set eyes and plush, girlish lips. He'd enlisted as a private but people who knew him felt confident he'd be promoted soon. He was educated, and persuasive when he chose to be. In the photographs taken before he left he never looks right into the camera, but off to the side a bit, chin slightly raised, eyes proud and purposeful.

My mother always told me that Tyson died at the Battle of Passchendaele. Maybe it's the sound of the word in English that made her remember it that way—the dramatic contrast between the hint of romance/passion and the knowledge that the battle left almost sixteen thousand Canadians dead, many of them buried forever beneath the Flanders mud. But she had it wrong. I've seen his military records: attestation papers declaring him faithful to King George the Fifth and the Canadian Over-seas Expeditionary Force; medical history (noting his maximum chest expansion was thirty-eight inches); pay sheets and service records. It is documented there that he was killed in action at Vimy, only a few days before the Canadian force successfully took the fabled ridge.

He had, indeed, been promoted. He made lance corporal while still in England and was named corporal after surviving the Battle of the Somme. In the month before his death, he was promoted to acting sergeant.

He probably considered his advancement up the ranks a mixed blessing. The Canadian troops were notoriously bitter about officers and staff, begrudging them their privileges. Even sergeants got to sleep separately from the men, had more leave time and ate in the officers' mess. The men didn't figure most of them deserved it. But Tyson would have been glad that the promotion meant more money sent home to his widowed mother.

In a letter of condolence the major of the battalion sent to Lillie a few days after Tyson's death, he wrote that he considered her son "a great personal friend." "His death was instantaneous," the major explained, "a shell killing him as he was getting his Machine Gun crew towards a Communication Trench." It was the morning of April 4, 1917, not quite a year since he'd been home.

The death of her son forced Lillie further into the solitude where she'd retreated after the wreck of the *Jones*.

People in Wiarton referred to her as an invalid, though she could get around perfectly well. She was said to have a delicate constitution.

The Crawford children who had left Wiarton by then made special trips home that summer after Tyson's death to stay at the lake with their mother. Lillie's brother Will had recently replaced the old family cottage at Petrel Point with a new one, and he and his brothers had set up a small log cabin for Lillie and the children just down the shore.

Lillie spent as much time there as possible. She would move over to the cabin the family called Kee-am as early as the weather allowed in spring, staying until it was so cold she could no longer sleep. The one-room building was rough-hewn and homey: lace curtains hung in the glassless windows; a table covered in white cotton would be set on the open porch, a jug full of ferns and wildflowers keeping the cloth from blowing away. There was no running water and only an outside privy. Eleanor, or one of the two youngest boys, Whit and Dick, would stay to look after their mother.

Lillie's nieces and nephews fondly remember those summers. They would listen to her play the organ and recite memorized verses at her side. They called her a dear, sweet soul. And her own children worshipped her. They regarded the time spent looking after her at Kee-am as if it were an honour.

I have a photograph of my great-grandmother taken near the cottage that seems to capture her perfectly. She's wearing a plaid fitted dress with a plain high collar and large covered buttons on the bosom. She doesn't look at the camera but you can see from her profile that her features are delicate, defined, almost birdlike. Her fine brown hair is brushed severely away from her face and drawn up into a scanty bun on top of her head. She's sitting on a lichen-covered rock on the sandy beach. There are pieces of driftwood and wildflowers at her feet, cedar trees behind. She is reading a book and appears oblivious to the photographer's presence. The picture itself isn't especially remarkable. The light is bad—it must have been an overcast day—and you can't see Lillie's face very well. But she is exactly as my grand-mother described her: engaged in the world of her books, slightly apart from the scene.

Of her father, my grandmother remembered nothing. She was only eighteen months old when the *Jones* disappeared. Later, when she began to comprehend the ways in which the wreck and her father's death had affected her life and the life of her town, she had little to go on. Lillie didn't talk about it, and the sentimental articles published in the local paper meant little to her. All she had were the rumours and stories—those she was told and those she made up to make sense of it all.

Her siblings helped fill in some of the blanks, though as the baby of the family, she never had much in common with them. Her eldest brother, Bert, was gone; Tyson was beloved, but absent as well, and then dead. Though Eleanor adored Madge, the only other girl in the family, and got along with Whit, they were much older, eleven and eight years, respectively—nearly the distance of a genera-tion. Even Dick, born in 1902 and closest to Eleanor in age, was like a foreign creature to her. In fact, she liked him least of all.

Her siblings remembered, as she did not, when their father was an important, influential man in Wiarton and their family name commanded respect. Eleanor never knew a time when they weren't poor, relying on the goodwill and charity of their extended family, on money sent home by the oldest children. There was never enough for the clothes she admired in women's magazines that belonged to her friends, or for the books she consumed with a passion equalled only by her mother. What had once been permanent was now fugitive, a shout in the wind. Their fall from grace made them all vulnerable.

Each year as the raging fall winds rolled in off the open water, as the bay turned wicked and cold, the anniversary of the wreck of the *Jones* was marked. Flags flew at half-mast. "In Memoriam" notices would crop up in the *Echo*. The *Jones* was always noted in some way—a photograph, an article—and was invariably referred to as Wiarton's greatest tragedy, one of the terrible mysteries of Georgian Bay. There was no escape from the shadow it cast.

In Eleanor's poetry and writing, her sense of herself as an outsider is clear. She felt the community's condemnation of her father sharply. The older people watched her, she was certain, waiting for her to confirm their suspicions about her family. If she shrieked too loudly flying down the hill on a toboggan it was sure to get back to her mother or Aunt Susie. If she lingered with a boy after school, she was an unconscionable flirt. If she failed to listen intently to a teacher, it was a sign of her disregard for the values of the town. Her father existed like a rumour, never quite real but always present, infecting everything, accompanying her each time she sat at the kitchen table or in her mother's room, when she walked across the beach into town.

She scribbled her torment onto pages of loose-leaf paper:

> Tradition,
> Lightly held,
> Haunts my darker moods
> Why have I,
> The helpless product
> Of heredity,
> Only displayed those qualities
> Which least adorned
> Illustrious progenitors?
> What matter?
> I will scoff on
> And laugh—
> Die laughing
> I am a Mendelian sport

Or this unfinished poem scrawled in pencil around the same time:

> Reluctantly the door to life swung wide
> A brown-eyed girl child came upon the stage
> Unwanted, resented, here to abide
> To feel, to dream, to grow within the cage
> And hope whereby she entered lingered on
> To paint the vista of unguided years

Eleanor felt even more alone once Whit left Wiarton for the United States. She and Dick fought bitterly. All her life my grandmother angrily remembered the times Dick forced her to climb the newly installed electrical poles that had brought light to Petrel Point. She climbed and climbed, shaking with fear that she might sizzle to death at any moment.

Lillie was too ill or, perhaps, too consumed by her own torment to notice. She regularly attended services and prayer meetings at the Baptist church where the Crawfords had moved when the Disciples church closed its doors. People in the congregation admired Lillie for her calm and her Christian forbearance, but to her youngest child, she was elusive. An absence. Eleanor longed to get her attention. But it was Lillie's sister Susie who became her surrogate mother.

Unmarried and childless, Susan Louise Tyson was an unlikely matriarch. When people in the family speak of her, she is always described as a maiden aunt. A creature unique to a certain pre-feminist time and place, the maiden aunt generally had little choice in the matter of her familial role. She would care for aging parents and sick siblings, she would take on the responsibility of looking after orphaned nieces and nephews. It was her Duty.

Susie was no exception. When the *Jones* went down, she was called upon to help out her oldest sister. When her father, Albert, died in the fall of 1912, she was expected to stay home to look after her mother, Bess. Thirty-one years old at the time, Susie—who had attended the Toronto Normal School and had done a year of domestic science at Guelph—had to put her own ambitions aside.

I was always told that Susie never married because she lost her fiancé in the Boer War. She was about the right age. And there were many men from the Orange Lodge–heavy Bruce Peninsula who enlisted with the

British army for service in South Africa. But the story is like many family tales: covered in a thin gloss of drama; shrouded in layers of other people's needs and hopes.

The truth is slightly more prosaic, though perhaps more devastating. Susie did lose a fiancé, but it was because she was forced to end the engagement. She met her beau at the Normal School. He was a smart boy, ambitious and well liked; they were to be married once he completed medical school. But when it became clear that it had fallen to Susie to care for her family, she broke it off. According to one version of the story, Susie's fiancé was so devastated by her decision that he vowed to marry the first woman who crossed his path.

In photographs from her youth, Susie is more handsome than beautiful. She wears her long black hair up in a soft roll. She has the skeptical eyes and mouth of an intelligent, serious young woman. She was an athlete when she was a girl, a founding member of the Wiarton women's hockey team. There's a picture of the turn-of-the-century team in a book of local history. Susie and the other young women sit poker-faced with their hockey sticks by their sides, dressed in wide dark tams, long skirts and stiff, high-necked white blouses. They are solemn. Their waists are tiny, their bodies shaped like wooden spindles.

As she grew older, Susie disdained sport and recreation for the church. She left the Tyson family pew at Frank Street Baptist for the Presbyterian congregation with its scourging psalms. Her God was a strict master, a disciplinarian.

Susie and her parents were also active in temperance work. Even after prohibition ended in Ontario in 1927,

Susie wouldn't let anyone drink in her presence. Brandy, she said, was a kind of medicine, but all other alcohol was strictly prohibited because it made men thieves and women harlots. (It became an open secret that Susie's brothers and nephews kept stashes of booze in the basement and shed at the house and beneath the stairs at the cottage. They would sneak away for a nip after Susie went to bed.)

It must have been a busy, exhausting life. Her mother was strong-willed and demanding, and lived until she was ninety-three. And when Susie's oldest brother, Will, lost his wife, Ada, in 1919, he and his three young daughters moved into the wide yellow-brick family home on Tyson Street. Susie helped raise the girls, looked after her brother and also cared for Lillie and her family, though the Crawfords lived on their own in a small house they found nearby.

Susie ran the family with an iron hand. She was rigid and controlling. She exercised her power with the children, demanding their attendance at church and their assistance around the house. She didn't hesitate to pronounce them lazy or thoughtless if they failed to live up to her expectations. She considered Eleanor to be particularly frivolous and full of airs, her head stuffed with nonsense, wasting her time with novels and her idle friends.

In photographs taken in the busy years when she was raising her two siblings' children and caring for her mother, Susie's eyes are tired-looking, deepened with dark circles. She began to pull her dark hair back into a more severe style. It emphasized the way her face had changed, the roundness that had once made her look full of possibility now carved into angles.

Susie was strict, but most members of the Tyson and

Crawford families also remember her as generous, with a great, dry sense of humour. She was the letter writer, staying in touch as her siblings, nieces and nephews fanned out across the country and the continent. It is her handwriting in the Tyson family bible that records the date and location of each person's birth, death and marriage. She kept the family together. The children and their parents were grateful for her sacrifices.

Perhaps they wouldn't even recognize the woman Eleanor would later describe as resentful, a cruel tyrant whose black hair never turned grey, whose righteous ways masked an anger more potent than brandy could ever cure. In a poem she wrote in her aunt's voice, Eleanor was unflinching.

Aunt Susie

Yes, I'm forty-one
And youth has gone.
I'm old
Or to-day I feel so.
My life has been freely
Given to a stern God and Duty.
All must be for the best, but why
Were life's feasts held from me?
I have loved
Yes loved deeply,
With more than youth's usual constancy.
But God pointed to Duty
In Mother's aging voice.
I do not complain
But she had husband and children

And Life has known my sisters,
Angie, wed to her Art,
Serene in a childless marriage;
Lillie with six children,
That I care for,
Hating them—not mine—
Then praying God forgiveness.
Now Mother, my anchor, is dying,
The children have grown
And gone.
What is left?
The blind lane of Duty seems ended.
This paper says there is no God!
Merciful Heaven!"

My grandmother never spoke about her childhood or about growing up in Wiarton without mentioning the malignant influence of her aunt Susie. She seemed to represent to Eleanor all that was wrong with the dutiful, self-denying emotional desert that was small-town Ontario. My grandmother told us one tale in particular that seemed to her to contain all that was necessary to know about her youth.

The story revolves around church, as so much did in the southern Ontario of her childhood. The Crawfords had been part of the Baptist church since before Eleanor was born, and though spontaneous conversion had been preempted by a tamer scripted ceremony (in which one accepted the fact of one's sinful nature and announced a willingness to submit to God), a conversion experience remained an important requirement. There were still those, of course, who came to the revelation suddenly—a bolt of lightning, a moment of grace. Roving ministers who travelled the countryside and set up tents to spread the gospel set aside time in their meetings for such moments. They'd sweep into town with their big awnings and booming voices and everyone—Methodists, Baptists, Presbyterians, even Anglicans—would troop in to watch. The thrilling theatrics of a revival tent preacher cut across the religious divide.

The way my grandmother told the story, it was a warm spring evening, the mildewed canvas of the tent flapping in the wind, when she went to a revival service with Aunt Susie and several of her cousins. There had been special meetings every night and afternoon over the previous week on subjects like "Manhood and Mastership," and "Shams, Hypocrisy, Lukewarmness, the Vanities of Life," but that night was the climax. With the long hibernation of winter over, people had come out in full force, filling the tent with their warm, musty breath.

Her best friend, Helen, was also there. The next day they would laugh at the holy rollers, imitating the dramatic gestures, the stagey rise and fall of the preacher's voice. "You are saved," they'd giggle, thumping each other on the forehead. But that night they couldn't find one another in the throng. Eleanor was forced to sit with her aunt. As they waited, the crowd sang popular hymns, the strained sopranos of the town's loudest singers drowning out the muddy shuffling of the less confident.

Then, my grandmother would later recall vividly, it was as if from nowhere that a tall, thin man came out of a fold in the tent. He cut off the singers abruptly with a voice that bounced off the canvas walls like an India-rubber ball.

And before she even got a chance to look around, to wiggle uncomfortably in her seat, to fix her best friend with a wicked smile that would set her off in fits of giggles, the preacher's attention came to rest on her head. Walking toward her, all eyes trained on his progress, he loudly declaimed, "Demons. This girl is beset by demons."

Splotchy red marks appeared on her neck and chin and she could feel the heat of Aunt Susie's glare, her darts of accusation.

"Let us pray for her," the preacher whispered dramatically, leaning on Eleanor's shoulder.

My grandmother never forgot what it felt like to have the eyes of every person in the tent boring holes into her skin. She longed to jump up and scream, to tear his hand away and run, yelling as she tore through the door. She wished she had the courage to denounce his cruel, self-righteous God, to turn to stone her duty-bound aunt. But she just boiled and fumed and sat eyes forward, motionless in her chair while the preacher moved on, the whole tent in the palm of his hand.

Helen Murphy made life in Wiarton bearable for Eleanor. In the photograph in the locket and in her albums Helen is a freckle-faced, rosy-cheeked blonde, boyish and full of fun. She and Eleanor look to be having a wonderful time, horsing around with a gaggle of other girls. They make faces and pose and hug one another near the beach at Kee-am and before the annual Empire Day parade in town. They're wearing snowshoes on the lake in winter, giggling in front of a dummy policeman in the middle of Berford Street in another. There's one of Eleanor and Helen and a bunch of friends balancing precariously on top of a metal post in the harbour. You can see the verdant south shore of Colpoy's Bay in the distance. In the border a caption in Eleanor's writing gleefully deems them "Freaks of Humanity."

They thought their hometown was dull, but they were determined not to be. During high school, Helen and Eleanor started doing an annual spring polar bear dip in Colpoy's Bay. Eleanor's brother Bert had made a big show of the same thing when he was a boy, preparing for weeks, collecting eggs and bread tickets and money for pork and beans to cook over a bonfire on the beach. But he and his friends hadn't dared to go in before the ice was totally gone. In 1922, Eleanor and Helen beat all records by plunging into the frigid water off Siemons dock on April 9. The ice that day was barely halfway to White Cloud Island. Shivering in their knee-length bathing suits and grinning like fools, they said that the water felt just grand. They'd had a "dilly time," they told the *Wiarton Echo*. Each year after that the *Echo* followed their ritual. "When the girls go in swimming we consider navigation has opened," the editor explained.

Eleanor also found escape in books—the untroubled constancy of words on a page. Her cousins remember her disappearing for whole days to read in the gazebo she'd convinced her uncles to build at the cottage. She wrote reams and reams of poetry, pouring her fears and doubts into her lined notebooks.

> It wasn't air I breathed; it was a poignant spell,
> Diffused of briar rose and dew.
> It wasn't sky I saw; it was a giant shell,
> A symphony in pastel hue.

The deep blue bay was all Tranquility.
The limestone cliff was all Stability.
The scene was one with me,
And I was part with it, but more than it could be.

Mother, what does it mean? Why can't I always seem
Complete and beautiful and glad?
Can life be like this promise, like this daytime dream?
Or is it nonsense, am I mad?
"Child, your mother is ill, be sensible.
Your conduct now is reprehensible.
All there is to beauty
Is work, and Christian charity, and duty."

"Ecstasy was yours, dear, but she brings her brother,
Pain the sculptor. You'll need to stay
True and sweet and strong—" "Yes, I hear you, Mother."
"—To travel their triumphant way.
Only a few of us are fashioned
To feel life with this impassioned
Awareness of meaning
And oneness in all things, and truth in dreaming."

Her writing got her mother's attention. Lillie encouraged her to keep at it. Eleanor hoped that one day she would leave Wiarton and prove herself smarter than the whole town. She would make her mother proud. In the books and newspapers she read she found glittering places of Beauty and Art, cafés spilling with laughter and conversation. She imagined herself far from the cold, looming cliffs of her hometown.

* * *

After I'd had my grandmother's locket for several years, it occurred to me one day that there might be something written on the back of the photographs enclosed there. A clue, a message, a signal from the past. As I'd delved deeper and deeper into Eleanor's life and her family story, it had become more clear to me what she had rejected in leaving Wiarton and her family. But there were many unanswered questions—perhaps even more than before.

I used a metal nail file to pry the locket open. The little gold frame around the pictures and the cover to protect them popped off easily. There was nothing written on the backs of the pictures, but behind each one, three more tiny photos were hidden.

One of the snapshots is of Eleanor and Helen; another is of Eleanor with an older man I didn't recognize, who is resting his arm proprietorially on her shoulder. The other four photos in the locket are all of young men. At least three of them looked familiar to me from the hours I'd spent engrossed in my grandmother's high school photo album. But the boy with the long head and big ears was the only one I could immediately identify. In her photo album, he's smiling and ruddy-faced, squeezed between Eleanor and Helen. He is identified as Soup.

I'd heard the name before. My mother had mentioned that someone named Soup was a good friend of Eleanor's, and the son of a prominent Wiarton man. Eleanor and Soup kept in touch their whole lives. My mother remembered visiting him and his young family when she was growing up in Montreal. Later, she went to nursing school with his daughter.

Soup was a tall, thin boy, almost exactly a year older than Eleanor. He had a trick knee after a runaway

Model T Ford knocked him down when he was sixteen years old. In high school, he and Eleanor and Helen thought of themselves as the Three Musketeers. They liked to get away from town, to slip through a crack in the fence near the cliffside mansion of a local politician and pluck tart red apples from the orchards there. They'd stay to watch the new electric lights in town sputter and start and the stars pop out of the circle of sky. Sometimes, late at night, they'd catch the flicker of a bonfire on the opposite shore, a signal to the bootlegger on White Cloud Island to send his hooch over in a rowboat.

But Soup's father was not just any old businessman, he was John Macaulay. Each year, as the anniversary of the wreck of the *Jones* was marked in the newspapers and churches of Wiarton, Eleanor and Soup were reminded of the tie—beyond friendship—that linked them.

The summer before Soup went off to university in Toronto, some local sailors put together the last of many search efforts for the *Jones*. It had been almost sixteen years since the steamer disappeared, but there were some men who were convinced that the hull would still be found on the bottom of Cove of Cork Bay, just north of Cape Croker.

One foggy Monday morning in July 1922, the captain of the *Henry Pedwell* left Owen Sound and headed for the little cove, expecting to meet up with another boat from Wiarton. He waited for a couple of hours but his fellow searchers were socked in by fog in Colpoy's Bay. The next week, two boats from Wiarton met the *Pedwell* at daybreak. From the stern of each boat the crew let out a towline attached to a single 900-foot steel cable. Almost as soon as they had released the cable, it caught on the bottom. But the object slipped away and the boats continued their search elsewhere in the cove. Later that day, they returned to the first spot and again the cable attached to something. The men were excited, certain that they had found the *Jones*. But by then the wind had come up and whitecaps made it difficult to get an accurate sounding or to determine what the object actually consisted of. The searchers took range measurements so they could find the location again and made plans to return the following week.

People in Wiarton and Owen Sound watched hawk-eyed at the docks. They scoured the newspapers for information about the search. But the boats never returned to the spot that summer. John Macaulay—who was still considered by people in Wiarton to be *the* authority on the *Jones*—voiced his opinion that Cove of Cork Bay was much too shallow to hold the steamer and that it had long ago slipped into a deeper part of the water or had been submerged on the muddy bottom. Searching would be for naught, he told anyone who asked. The effort was shelved for good.

Eleanor, Helen and Soup talked often about leaving Wiarton. They were ambitious, excited by the changes the world had seen in the years since the end of the war. For the girls, especially, the possibilities tempted like those stolen apples, ripe for the plucking. Women had won the right to vote in national elections. An Owen Sounder named Agnes McPhail had recently been elected to the Canadian Parliament, the first woman in the country's history. Even in Wiarton, girls were bobbing their hair, wearing short skirts and men's pants, smoking cigarettes.

The idea of this new, unencumbered woman was a powerful one for Eleanor. She wanted very much not to care about old-world expectations, about Aunt Susie and her rigid model of womanhood—devoted to "Christian charity and duty." In poems like "Villanelle," about the pirate in her family tree, Eleanor explored what it would be like to breezily ignore the restrictions of her family and her sex: to "break men's hearts so carelessly/Never give more than the littlest kiss. . . ."

The pirate had become both her torment and her talisman. Her father's responsibility for the wreck of the *Jones* cast a shadow over her and her family, but it was also oddly liberating. Thinking of herself as heir to an outlaw gave Eleanor permission to reject what she saw as the petty concerns of her insular hometown.

In the spring of 1924, Eleanor and Helen graduated from Wiarton High School. Eleanor finished at the top of her class in composition and literature. Everyone thought she would be a writer. Maybe a girl reporter. She made no secret of the fact that she planned to leave as soon as possible.

She hoped to go to university. Her mother had always encouraged it, though she hadn't the money to pay tuition. Marriage could definitely wait. Eleanor had never been interested in divining her future husband by the bounces of a ball or the petals of a flower. The young and very beautiful American poet Edna St. Vincent Millay had just been awarded the Pulitzer Prize for her anthems of free love in *A Few Figs from Thistles* and other books. Dorothy Parker was at the Algonquin Round Table in New York City, spouting pithy bons mots with some of the great male writers of her generation. Eleanor had read about the world outside Wiarton and defiantly imagined herself a part of it.

ↂ

October 26, 1924, Wiarton

Eleanor is packing. She's got four more days before she leaves for Baltimore and it's the fifth time she's packed. Each time, she lugs her heavy suitcase onto the bed and pulls everything out to start again. She pats the smooth pressed cotton of her white shirts and refolds the pleats in her skirts. She wishes she had better, more stylish clothes. She's going to wear her best outfit on the train—a drop-waist dress beneath a brown velvet coat and a sweet little cloche—but after that it's all just black woollen skirts and starchy shirts. People in Baltimore will think she's just off the turnip truck.

There's a knock at her door. "Hal-ooooo," Helen says, pushing into the room. She's flushed and breathing hard from running up the stairs. She goes over to the bed and flops down dramatically beside Eleanor's suitcase. "The train took even longer than usual. I'm drop-dead tired," she says.

Helen has been visiting her mother's sister in Toronto. Underneath her boxy winter coat she is wearing a new green wool skirt and top that her aunt must have bought for her. Her wavy blonde hair is cut in a short bob and held back with a barrette, but it's unruly, as usual, poking out at all angles, like straw.

"I can't believe you're packing. I can't believe you're

leaving me," Helen says, drawing herself up on her elbows. "I'm a loooooonesome lettle raaaaindrop," she sings in a fake falsetto.

Eleanor laughs and throws a pair of woollen socks at her friend. "You'll be leaving soon, too, you silly goose. You'll meet some fellow on the train to Toronto and have a brood of blue-eyed babies before I even get to Baltimore. I'll be the one who's all alone. Captive of my work." Eleanor puts her hand to her forehead and tilts her head back in a gesture of brave sorrow. "The lonely poet living on nothing but canned pork and beans, suffering for Art."

"Aw, shut up," Helen says and throws the black socks back at Eleanor. "With your powers of persuasion, you won't be suffering much."

"I don't even care if I do," Eleanor says as she flaps out a blouse and refolds it. "Nothing can be as bad as this place."

"I won't miss Wiarton. That's for sure. Or anyone in it. Present company excepted, of course." Eleanor grins at her friend, who gives a single, purposeful nod.

"And Susie, of course." Helen smirks.

"Ha. Ha. Very funny," says Eleanor. "You're a regular Charlie Chaplin. Say, did I tell you that Madge wants to be called Peggy now? That's what Richard calls her and she says I should, too, since I'm going to be living with them."

Eleanor presses her one pair of pants into the suitcase. "It's going to be strange," she says quietly, as if talking to herself.

Helen lifts herself off the bed and walks over to a stack of books Eleanor has arranged on a low stool ready for packing. She picks up *The Rubaiyat of Omar Khayyam*, which their friend Gretchen gave Eleanor as a farewell gift. The illustrations are beautiful, richly coloured and passionate.

"A Book of Verses underneath the Bough,/ A Jug of Wine, a Loaf of Bread—and Thou . . ." Helen reads, then snaps the book shut, pretending to be shocked. "I don't imagine Susie would like the look of this one," she says, raising her eyebrows.

"My thoughts precisely." Eleanor smiles and tucks the book into the small fabric bag she'll carry on the train.

She folds her last skirt into the suitcase and reluctantly closes the latch. Packing keeps her mind from straying. She never would have thought she'd be worried about going, not when getting out of Wiarton is the thing she's wanted as long as she can remember. But whenever she stops for a moment it's there, digging holes in her certainty.

Eleanor lifts the bulky suitcase and parks it behind the door. Helen has moved over to the small dresser on the other side of the room and is sitting in front of the mirror trying to pat down her hair. Eleanor joins her, leaning over her friend to look at her own reflection. Cheeks a little too chubby. Baby fat, still. Hair too curly—she can never keep it straight for very long. Lips are all right, though a hint of rouge would make them stand out more. Eleanor pulls her hair back off her face to look more closely at her skin. People have always said she looks Spanish with her olive skin and dark hair. Not for the first time, she imagines that she was adopted, left on the doorstep to be raised by the Crawford family.

"So what does your mother think of it all?" Helen asks, looking up in the mirror. "I mean, she'll really miss you."

"It was Mother's idea that I live with Madge, uh, I mean Peggy." Eleanor smiles at her gaffe. "You know that. She even borrowed money from my uncle. She wants me to go."

"But now that you're really going, it's different. For all of us."

"Don't fuss, darling," Eleanor says, patting down Helen's hair. "When I'm a famous poet I'll still come to visit you and Mother. They'll string banners across the streets to welcome me and I'll wave like the viscountess to the little people." Eleanor does an exaggerated flutter of her hand and her friend grins.

The shadows are lengthening in the room and it's getting harder to see in the mirror. Helen stands up, smooths her skirt and heads for the door. "I've got to be home before dinner. I promised Mother I'd help," she says.

Eleanor gives another royal wave as she sits down in the chair that Helen has vacated: "Ta-ta for now."

She can hear Helen's feet on the creaky stairs, then the side door open and close as she heads out on the street. Eleanor lies down on her narrow bed. She stares at the cracks in the ceiling and traces the stitching on her quilt with one finger. She knows instinctively where the thread is missing, where she can slip her whole hand beneath the fabric star. She's had this quilt her entire life.

Eleanor hums "I'm a lonesome little raindrop" to herself. But her anxiety is stubborn. *What if I don't get into school or find work at a newspaper or sell some of my poems to the magazines. What if? What if?* It goes around in her head like a movie reel showing the same picture again and again in an endless loop.

Eleanor stands up and goes over to the window. She can see Helen disappearing up the street. "Ta-ta," she whispers. It's only 5 p.m. and it's nearly pitch dark. The days are getting shorter and shorter. There's barely any daylight in this godforsaken town.

Berkeley, California, was about as far from her little hometown as Eleanor had ever hoped to be.

Chapter 13

IN A STRANGE LAND

WHEN ELEANOR WENT TO BALTIMORE to live with her sister, Peggy, and her husband, Richard, they had only been married a year or two. I have a photograph of Peggy that was taken for the wedding. She's seated, dressed in a white gown, holding a rose at her waist, her shoulders covered in a cloud of gauzy white tulle. She has crimson lips, startling eyes much like her mother's, and pale, smooth skin.

Peggy was a nurse. She'd trained in Baltimore, and met Richard, a doctor, when she was stationed in

Berkeley with the U.S. Army Nursing Corps during the war. He was German, from a family that counted Sigmund Freud among its intimates; he'd become a Freudian disciple.

When Eleanor arrived in Baltimore, Peggy and Richard were already planning to return to California, where he had been offered a job. It worked out well for all of them. Eleanor would apply to the university at Berkeley. Within the year, they were headed across the continent by train.

In January 1926, Eleanor registered at the University of California at Berkeley in the College of Letters and Sciences. It was about as far from her hometown as she had ever hoped to be. Nestled into the Berkeley hills, the dry, dusty town had soaring pines and fragrant eucalyptus trees, the salty flavour of San Francisco Bay in the air. From the window of the little bedsit she found near the university, Eleanor could see the Campanile, a 300-foot white granite clocktower that looms over the valley like a Tuscan sentry.

The university gave the little town a flicker of sophistication but it was San Francisco, built on myth and gold, an hour across a shark-infested bay and teeming with people from all over the world, that held Eleanor in its thrall. There was the Palace Hotel on Market Street with its dusky corners and low ceilings, the air hazy with smoke and sweat and saxophones. On Fridays, college students got a discount at the door. Some of the more adventurous would head to the wild Barbary Coast district lit up by gaslights, where cheap Italian restaurants had set up in the place of dives and cabarets and brothels. Or the steep, cobblestone alleys of

Chinatown, where students sneaked a look through latticed windows at the chop suey joints hidden behind.

Eleanor was amazed and cowed by the sophistication of her fellow students. The girls rolled their stockings and smoked cigarettes in holders, the boys read ironic, saucy magazines like *Judge* and *Life* and *College Humour.* There were Communists selling radical newspapers on campus and poets reading in coffeehouses. The year she enrolled at Berkeley, the campus literary magazine, *The Occident,* was embroiled in a fight for freedom of speech after the writer of an article deemed to contain "immoral and sacrilegious material" was deprived of his scholarship and accused in newspapers across the country of being in the pay of the Bolsheviks. The short story, which depicted Joseph angry with God for impregnating his wife, was "seized on the press and subsequently suppressed," according to an editorial in a guerrilla edition of the magazine published off-campus. Even students who were appalled by the sentiment of the story protested against the breach of the right to free speech. It was the principle of the thing.

Eleanor's time at Berkeley had an enormous impact on her. There were people she knew later in life who thought she'd grown up in California she talked about it so much.

Out of curiosity, I sent away for her university transcripts. The form, filled in by hand, listed her first-year courses as physical education, English, zoology, philosophy and general literature. The transcript notes her withdrawal on May 12, 1926, and a leave of absence granted a week later. I was surprised to learn that she'd dropped out after barely finishing her first term.

There would have been lots of reasons for Eleanor to leave school. University was expensive. She had to work as an office girl at a perfume company on First Street in San Francisco to help pay her tuition and expenses. She typed and filed and fetched coffee. Much of her poetry from that time is on letterhead with "Paul Rieger & Company, High Grade Perfumes" inscribed at the top.

And her grades were disappointing. One of her very first papers came back with a big red C+ scarred on its back. It was demoralizing to find herself mired in mediocrity when she had always been an A student.

In an essay she submitted to her English class titled "My Difficulties in Writing," she explained:

> If your mother is a writer of some local importance and your uncle an editor of the locality's weekly paper; if your English teacher is fond of bridge and your mother's teas are locally famous, then a strange and seemingly irrelevant conclusion is reached. You have no difficulties in writing. Three neat pages about rippling brooks and sighing winds bring a mark of ninety-five from a possible hundred.
>
> But the circumstances have altered. The infant prodigy is in a strange land where the editor and the teas are unknown, where to read of rippling brooks and sighing winds is to yawn. . . .
>
> Then, my difficulties increase directly with my feeling for the subject. A mildly interesting subject shapes itself without confusion or regret to earn the regulation C. To feel deeply is to despair of expression. First, I half begrudge the release of a thought from intimate depths, but that is forgotten in my angry chase for words, adroit words, to clothe it. . . . Gingham is ready at hand sometimes when the exotic life needs

satin. . . . And I will have failed to put my idea into life.
In the hopeless banality, my eyes alone of all the world
can perceive the ghost of a delightful subtlety.

Eleanor wondered if her grades would be better if she didn't
have to work. And she couldn't forgive the pretty sorority
girl who conspicuously moved her chair to sit beside
another classmate who wore prettier clothes and got higher
marks. It made her wonder if she was cut out for school,
for a career as a writer. Her skin was too thin.

"Having been reared on my dear aunt's violent morality,
I fear my senses have been blunted to decent and kind
treatment," Eleanor scrawled on the back of one of her
assignments, ending abruptly, as if she planned to say
more. She began to doubt everything she had ever believed
about herself—maybe Aunt Susie had been right, and her
talent was nothing more than pretension.

Eleanor turned to her sister for comfort. Peggy and
Richard lived in Palo Alto, only a few hours down the
road from Berkeley, and she visited whenever she could.
Eleanor adored and respected her sister but she came to
fear Richard. When she spoke of him to my mother and
aunt, she said that he made "advances." She never told
Peggy about it.

All of it together—the costs and her unsatisfying
grades, her brother-in-law's behaviour—must have rattled
Eleanor. She decided she couldn't stay in California any
longer. Once she was granted a leave from UC Berkeley,
she headed back to Wiarton to spend the summer of 1926.

I puzzled for a long time at my grandmother's decision
to return to the town she had been so desperate to leave
only two years before, until I realized that there was

another piece to the story, a piece that my grandmother never acknowledged when she talked about her Berkeley days. Perhaps it just didn't fit into the tale she'd chosen to tell about herself, but when she abruptly left California in the spring of 1926, she had just accepted a marriage proposal from a boy back home.

Fritz Knechtel was the third son of a furniture magnate from Hanover, Ontario, a prosperous town of mostly German immigrants southwest of Wiarton. Since his grandfather, Daniel Knechtel, formed the eponymous furniture firm in the 1880s, the Knechtels had been one of the most prominent families in the region. By the late 1920s the company was not only Hanover's largest employer, it was a significant landholder with a four-storey factory on the main street, a second office-furniture plant in town, plus factories in Walkerton and Southampton and a warehouse in Winnipeg. Daniel Knechtel financed Hanover's hospital, library, park and YMCA. But the elder Knechtel lived frugally, collecting an hourly salary and priding himself on owning a home that was no more grand than one his workmen could afford. He thought of himself as a craftsman, not a capitalist.

Fritz's father, Jacob, was Daniel's oldest son. He took over management of the company once his father relinquished active leadership. But Jacob, known as J.S., was different from his father. He had been to business college and studied French at a Baptist mission in Quebec. He was also a painfully shy man, more interested in technical details than hands-on woodworking. And unlike his father, he was happy to embrace the luxuries the family's money and prestige bought. There was a summer home on the Lake Huron shore, a winter estate at Del Ray Beach in Florida and the Tamarac Island Fishing and Shooting Club at Stoke's Bay on the east coast of the Bruce Peninsula. He and his wife and children lived well, as befitted the wealthiest, most important family in town.

Like many of the other second- and third-generation German immigrants in Hanover, the Knechtels still spoke German inside their home. Their Baptist church held services in German and taught German vocabulary in the Sunday school. Rosalina, J.S.'s wife, was of the old school. She was strong-minded and rigid, remembered as having sole dominion over the family when they were in her home. Much was expected of her five children.

After leaving high school in Hanover, Fritz attended McMaster, then a Baptist college on the University of Toronto campus. When he graduated, he was offered a position as a Montreal-based salesman for the family company.

Fritz and Eleanor met when she was in high school. The young people in the little towns of the Bruce Peninsula and farther south often socialized together at church and community social events. And, Fritz had friends in Wiarton. He spent a lot of time at the family cottage in nearby Oliphant.

It's hard to know when their friendship became something more—though I finally realized after staring at it that Fritz's picture is one of the ones hidden in my grandmother's locket. In the photograph he is younger than I'd seen him before; he's wearing a newsboy's cap, his trademark round glasses and a short, narrow moustache. It's an odd photograph because the way Eleanor cut it out there's more overexposed white background than person.

He seems shrunken and insubstantial, sliding off the left-hand bottom edge.

To people who knew them together, Eleanor and Fritz seemed an unlikely pair. Eleanor was ambitious and vivacious. Fritz was a serious, quiet young man, a few years older. He wore round glasses, had a high forehead and thinning blond hair, which made him look a lot like his father. He spoke with the slightest hint of a German accent and was interested in Native Canadian artifacts.

But Fritz's offer of marriage must have been compelling to Eleanor. He was kind and generous with her, and he had prospects. The year she returned to Canada, the Knechtel Furniture Company had posted record profits. Fritz's father had recovered from a prolonged illness—pneumonia, combined with a nervous breakdown had kept him bedridden for nearly three years—in time to see the economy kick into high gear. In the mid to late 1920s, the furniture manufacturing industry as a whole saw unprecedented growth.

With no money and only one term of college completed, her confidence in her writing and herself shaken, Eleanor needed a way out. The promise of a life free from financial worries, the instant status conveyed upon her as the wife of a Knechtel and a new chance to make a life in Montreal must have seemed to Eleanor like her last, best chance.

She knew she didn't love Fritz. He was a comrade, an intellectual sparring partner. In a poem she wrote to him when she was still in California, she teased him about relying on the values of the past:

The world which stops prize-fights,
And howls for war;
And calls pacifists fools,
Urging force as the great nobility,
Then crucifies workmen who use force,
And says that nothing is gained by force;
And preaches love, and robs the weak—
All this insane, topsy-turvy, aimless,
Witless talking and childishness,
This woman mind,
This insane world!
Who can say,
This is right, that is wrong.

Raised in a house where notions like right and wrong were as obvious as the hat on his head, Fritz must have puzzled at her question. But by all accounts, he adored her. He may have known or suspected Eleanor didn't love him in quite the same way, but it was of little consequence. Once she became his wife, she would surely take on the role gladly. Eleanor must have wanted very much to believe him.

At the end of June 1926, Helen Murphy's mother threw a shower for the young bride-to-be. There was confetti and tiny presents tied with bows, verses "wise and unwise," according to the notice in the newspaper. The wedding itself was held just over a month later on a hot August afternoon in Wiarton's Baptist Church. Ministers from both the Wiarton and Hanover churches presided. Helen Murphy was Eleanor's attendant. Her brother Whit walked her down the aisle to the strains of Lohegrin's wedding march. The *Echo* reported that the bride's gown of white crepe was "trimmed with cobwebs of rhinestones." The *Hanover Post* noted that a Limerick lace veil was held from her face with a bandeau of orange blossoms. Standing at the front of the church, Eleanor held a bouquet of pink sweetheart roses. In her other hand, she clutched the lace handkerchief her great-aunt Jane had made for her mother's wedding so long ago. Eleanor hoped it would bring her better luck.

In the photographs of Eleanor and her son, Peter, there's that elusive summer glow about them—the blur of long, warm days that always end too soon.

Chapter 14

As Man and Wife

MY GRANDMOTHER RETURNED TO WIARTON as infrequently as possible after she married Fritz and moved to Montreal. The two of them found an apartment on Bloomfield Avenue in Outremont and set up a modest home. Fritz travelled a lot for work. He'd often be gone for two weeks at a time, trolling the back roads of rural Quebec selling furniture to small stores and dealers. Asked to list his occupation, he wrote "traveller."

Later my grandmother would remember with a laugh

that in her first few days in Montreal she thought the giant illuminated cross on top of Mount Royal was an apparition, a taunting ghost from her past reminding her of her ungodly ways. But she soon became enamoured with the city—Canada's largest at the time—with its cobblestone streets by the harbour and dense, forested green space rising up in the middle. In her poetry she even admitted a grudging admiration for Montreal's signature crucifix: "And from the cross, downhill, into the night/ There seem to spill and scatter, wand'ring stars,/ And then a thousand streets of yellow light,/ Bright growling trams and the swift slur of cars."

She registered at McGill University to complete her bachelor's degree. In her scrapbook she stuffed programs and notices from campus events she attended. She and her new friends explored the city together. There was La Corona, Canada's own Algonquin Hotel where famous actors and actresses in town for a show, chorus girls and local musicians mingled to drink and flirt. The flickers played at any number of movie palaces. Eleanor watched sculpted palaces of blue ice rise up on Fletcher's Field in the winter and learned the arcane rules of a city divided into distinct and inviolable worlds: one French, another English. She slid into the slipstream of the city of nearly one million people. Immigrants were making Montreal more and more cosmopolitan, and with her dark hair and brown eyes she didn't correct those who assumed she was part Mexican or Native American.

Fritz rarely joined Eleanor in these explorations. He was around so infrequently that she often didn't tell her new friends that she was married. Occasionally she went even further, passing him off as her older brother. It was a terrible deceit, but it was also, perhaps, how she saw him. She felt herself too young to be married to a travelling salesman, a man saddled with responsibilities and expectations, old before his time.

Eleanor was so thoroughly dislodged from her past, from her life in the little town on Georgian Bay, that when her mother suddenly fell ill at the end of November 1926, it was a shock to have to confront it again.

Lillie hadn't been strong for years, of course. Not since her stroke, not since Jim died, since Tyson was killed in action. But she got around. She still went to regular prayer meetings and spent most of the summer at Kee-am.

She was just a week shy of her fifty-ninth birthday when she had her last stroke. The children came pouring home from all over Canada and the U.S. to keep vigil at her bedside. Lillie floated in and out of consciousness for five days. She seemed to respond only when her children read poetry to her. Then, according to the story Eleanor often told, early one morning Lillie Tyson Crawford took her last breath lying in her youngest daughter's arms.

My grandmother was twenty-one years old when Lillie died. But the way she spoke of it later when she told the story to her two daughters, she was just a child, a helpless, orphaned girl left alone in the world. She felt abandoned all over again.

Fritz never appeared in Eleanor's story about Lillie's death. Perhaps he was held up in Montreal on business, waiting to hear that his mother-in-law had recovered. Or maybe, once again, he didn't fit into Eleanor's story about herself. Fritz was a bespectacled enigma, stone-faced and silent in most of her tales. He smoked like a chimney and had a bad temper. Even this she didn't mention often.

She had almost nothing to say about their marriage or even their estrangement and divorce nine and a half years later. In fact, she didn't tell my mother and my aunt Paula about her first marriage until they were teenagers. And then, most shocking of all, she revealed that she had had a child with this first husband. They had a brother.

Eleanor was depressed after her mother died at Christmas 1926. Once she got back to Montreal, she didn't have the heart to return to McGill. She dropped out and stayed home in the little apartment where she lived with Fritz, writing poems like this one she called "Failure."

> There is a town on Georgian Bay
> That tired, leans against a hill,
> Her head held high, while soiled feet stay
> Down in the mire by the mill.
>
> A sleepy street has an abrupt
> Meeting, it seems, with tow'ring rock
> But a tortuous path winds up
> To the old steps of wooden block.
>
> Youth's gay, adventurous spirit
> Called the cliff-side an easy slope;
> And the mind that did not fear it,
> Asked for higher hazards to cope.
>
> Lying flat on rain-washed limestone
> I planned the years that were to be,
> The splendid deeds that could be done
> When my climbing would make me free.

I dreamed that I would pause at last,
The ultimate slope at my feet,
And I could help those I had passed
To gain a more exalted seat.

The human mind cannot maintain
With ease, the heights that thought can plan;
And on a rarified, high plane
The earth's less firm to feet that ran.

I was a fool to build beyond
The tired town that gave me birth.
I would I could lose this strange wan
Cheek, and regain the old, glad mirth.

I would not ask for hills to scale
I would lean like a town I see,
On ageless strength that cannot fail,
My feet in mud, head high and free.

She was miserable. She saw her mother as the only person who had ever encouraged her. With Fritz away on Knechtel Furniture business all the time, she felt utterly alone. She began to resent him his work, even his interaction with other people.

Like Lillie, Eleanor began to clip articles and poems that she pasted into a big black scrapbook. A magazine piece called "The Story of Happiness" by Will Durant caught her eye with its admonishment to "Follow your own bent, pursue your curiosity bravely, express yourself, make your own harmony. . . ." On the opening pages of her book she glued two illustrations, one of a big, rambling house surrounded by wildflowers and grasses, another of a pretty garden gate. Beneath the house she glued a quote from Emily Dickinson: "There is no frigate like a book / To take us lands away. . . ."

Then, slowly, she gathered her resources. She got involved in volunteering at McGill University's settlement house, a centre for new immigrants, and began to go out with her friends again. She even started to consider a career in journalism. An unsigned letter from a friend that she kept for the rest of her life gave her new conviction:

> Let me remind you of your ability to deal with journalistic affairs. I would pursue it in your place. Please do not stagnate. We are living in an age the world, I dare say, never saw before. And to be acutely aware of the tremendous changes undergoing in our social code at the present time is an asset. You have the mind to grasp them, you have due to that knowledge made use of them. . . .

There were other women writing for magazines and newspapers in Montreal. Even married women. *The Chatelaine—A Magazine for Canadian Women* had just been launched to great fanfare. It was the late 1920s. Montreal was booming. Skyscrapers were being built. Hockey was king. People were rich and spending money like water.

But then, late in the spring of 1928, Eleanor discovered that she was pregnant. The baby was due the following winter. There could be no question of going back to school or looking for work.

Peter Tyson Knechtel was born in February 1929 at the Royal Victoria Hospital in Montreal. He was healthy, all chubby cheeks and rosebud lips. In the tired haze of caring for an infant, Eleanor didn't even mind that she wasn't writing a word. It was all she could manage to feed and tend the baby and look after their small home.

Only a few months after Peter's birth, the depression knocked the Knechtels and the rest of the country off their feet. Just as it had burned more brightly than other industries in the late 1920s, furniture manufacturing crashed more precipitously. No one was buying new household goods, and the rise of unionized shops had changed the balance of power in the factories. After the fall of 1929, the fortunes of the Knechtel Furniture Company went downhill and stayed there for a decade.

Fritz became sullen and withdrawn as he and the family company struggled to survive the economic nosedive. Bills began to pile up. They seemed to be short of money all the time. As Peter got older and became more independent, Eleanor craved space to herself. She wanted a chance to write, to get out of the house alone occasionally. But Fritz was too consumed by worry and fear to notice. Perhaps he found out that some of Eleanor's friends thought that he was her brother or she confessed in a flash of fury that she found him dull, that she had never loved him. Whatever the cause, Fritz decided to assert himself, to exercise his husbandly privileges. She would have a clean house and dinner on the table when he got home. She had a duty to him and their child. There would be no more parties or frippery with her friends. Eleanor felt like an inmate in her home.

*   *   *

In her bedroom, my mother keeps a vanity set that once belonged to Eleanor. There is a sterling-silver hairbrush and a hand-held mirror, a real tortoiseshell comb, a nail buffer and a delicate crystal jar with a silver lid. All are incredibly heavy. Even now when I pick up the mirror, the top weaves precariously back and forth in my grip.

On all of the pieces a loopy "K" is engraved in the silver. The set was a wedding gift at Eleanor's marriage to Fritz in 1926. She kept them after her divorce because they were given to her by Helen Murphy's family. Once she married my grandfather, Paul, and they started their own family together, the set must have been a bittersweet reminder of the life she'd left behind.

The story I've always heard about Eleanor and Fritz's divorce—the account my grandmother told her daughters once she decided they were old enough—was that she left Fritz when she couldn't take his anger anymore. Once, she said, he chased her with a knife, threatening to kill her if she didn't come back. She had never loved him, she told the girls; things were never easy.

Eleanor said that she was introduced to their father, Paul, by his sister Ruth, whom she'd known when they were at McGill together. When Eleanor was looking for a divorce lawyer, Ruth had apparently suggested her brother could take care of it. According to this oft-repeated story, Eleanor and Paul fell in love over long, difficult days of legal work.

It would have been hard not to fall in love with Paul Smith. He had the broad-shouldered good looks of a matinee idol, and an athlete's ease with his body. He'd been a star defenceman with the champion varsity hockey team at McGill; president of his undergraduate law class. There was talk about him playing professional hockey, but he got injured and couldn't continue. A couple of photographs taken of him in the late 1920s have always seemed to me to exemplify the Jazz Age: jaunty hat perched at an angle, huge beaverskin coat swinging as he strides along a Montreal high street.

Paul Smith was definitely a man of his time: a flawed but confident character straight out of a Hemingway novel, serious about himself and brusque. He liked to hunt wild animals, smoke a cigar and down a stiff drink. His friends were important young men, lawyers and capitalists, hockey players like Montreal Maroons legend Hooley Smith, the Bad Boy of Balmy Beach.

People who worked with him remember my grandfather as a ferocious lawyer. He would serve twelve years on the council of the city of Montreal and would be named to the King's Counsel before he turned forty. To his family, he was a difficult but loving man. He was happiest when he was out in the bush.

Eleanor wasn't the first woman to fall for him. His early photo albums are filled with pictures of waifish girls, flappers with bobbed hair and boyish figures wearing drop-waist dresses and hats pulled down low. There was one girl in particular whom he dated for a number of years in high school and into university. Her name was Blanche and she was the scion of a wealthy local family; she was pretty, with delicate features and fashionable clothes. In his scrapbook she wears a Persian lamb coat in one photo, a skiing costume in another; elsewhere she's sitting on a low part of the walled garden at his family's home; in another photo she's standing grimly on board what looks to be an ocean liner.

Everyone said they would marry. When he dragged his feet about popping the question, she took matters into her own hands and published an engagement announcement in the local newspaper. Perhaps she thought he would find it funny, but she had greatly underestimated my grandfather's temper. He was so furious at what he took to be her manipulation that he immediately ended the relationship. His family was shocked, but they knew not to press the subject when he shot a bullet through the oil portrait his mother had painted of the girl.

When my mother was little, she and her cousins liked to sneak off to the attic at the Smith family home to look at the punctured picture, fingering the hole and telling one another exaggerated tales of a doomed love affair.

Of their own love affair, Eleanor told her daughters that she and their father liked to read poetry to one another. When they were dating, they would go motoring together in his big black car with wide runners along the side.

The story of their mother's divorce and the existence of a half-brother was shocking to my mother and aunt, particularly since divorce was still rare in the late 1950s. But they also thought it deeply romantic. After what she described to them as a difficult, orphan childhood, they saw her as having escaped, tearing herself free from the clutches of an ogre to find a prince. She seemed exotic to them, more beautiful than ever, a sort of modern Cinderella.

Thinking I might uncover some more details about this romance, I set out to find the record of Eleanor and Fritz's divorce. I quickly discovered that my task was not going to be an easy one. Eleanor and Fritz didn't get their divorce in Quebec as I had assumed, and I could find nothing in the two-foot-high casebooks from the Wiarton and Hanover–area courts. That left me to scroll through names and accusations scribbled in record books for each of Ontario's counties until I could locate the correct name and case number. Many trips to the archives later I finally came across a notation in the Middlesex County casebook. It read *Knechtel v. Knechtel and Smith*.

When the archivist called after several days to tell me the papers I'd requested had been retrieved from storage, I raced over to the reading room at the Archives of Ontario in downtown Toronto. I was instructed to wear white gloves and keep the documents in the manila folder in order. It was exciting; no one else had ever asked to see the file before. For once, I imagined, I'd found a story unchanged by the passage of time, free from memory's tricks of omission and emphasis.

The file was thick, bound with string and heavy with legalese. The documents were typed, stamped and signed but the formality couldn't disguise the ugly account of a marriage gone sour. It didn't take more than a few minutes to figure out that nearly everything I'd been told about my grandmother's divorce was wrong.

It was Fritz, it turned out, not my grandmother, who filed for divorce on September 3, 1935, asking for the dissolution of his marriage to Eleanor Jane Knechtel. He asked the court to do so on "the grounds of [her] adultery with the Defendant Paul S. Smith, and on the grounds of desertion. . . ." My grandfather had not been Eleanor's lawyer, after all. He'd been her lover.

I had to reread the whole package several times to get my head around what it contained. Each time I felt less excited by my discovery, more uncomfortable, as if I were a rubbernecker at the scene of an accident. I wasn't sure any longer that I even wanted to know the sordid details of this deception. It made me realize that there are consequences not only for forgetting one's history, but for remembering it.

According to interviews contained in the divorce documents, things began to really unravel for Fritz and Eleanor when Peter was three years old and they moved out of Montreal to the nearby suburb of Woodlands. The depression had exacted a heavy toll on the family, and Fritz and Eleanor were financially strained enough that they decided to take in boarders at their new house in order to help pay the bills. Eleanor's old friend Soup Macaulay, who'd recently moved to Montreal, took one room, and she rented out two others to strangers. Eleanor cooked for the boarders and took care of the house.

At first she hated it. A few years before, being a landlady would have been out of the question for a married, middle-class woman. There were still people around who considered a boarding house akin to a brothel. Women who kept them were watched carefully. They were considered to have more opportunity than most for depraved behaviour.

But Eleanor soon discovered that she liked running the house. She loved to cook, experimenting with ingredients and recipes. And with Fritz either angry or away on business all the time, having people around meant she wasn't lonely. There were masquerade parties at the house and happy days holding court on the great big porch, its roof held up by pillars.

In the divorce proceedings, my grandparents admit that it was then that they became romantically involved. They'd met, each explained in separate interviews contained in the record, in 1929, not long after Peter was born. Paul's sister, Ruth, had indeed introduced them, but it was during a weekend at the Smith family home in the Ottawa Valley northwest of Montreal. Fritz and Eleanor had been invited to visit and Paul happened to be home from his law studies at McGill.

Ruth and Paul's father, Walter Smith, was a doctor who'd started a private hospital in the town of Hawkesbury, Ontario. He and his wife lived in a gracious old stone house called Duldreaggan Hall, built by a fur trader in the early 1880s. Surrounded by green lawns with gnarled oaks and soaring pine trees, the house had a stunning view of the Ottawa River and the Laurentian Mountains. But perhaps the most remarkable thing about the property was the beautifully tended walled garden thick with lilies and roses, peonies and delphiniums half the height of the house. There was a small pond with electric-yellow water lilies floating on the surface, trellises made of twisted branches with sweet peas winding up the limbs, benches dotted here and there around the garden and the expanse of lawn. Ruth and Paul's mother, May, tended this garden and was a formidable presence in her own right.

Eleanor must have fallen in love with the family as soon as she and Fritz drove up the long winding driveway. The house and the garden gate looked uncannily like the illustrations she had pasted in her scrapbook in those lonely days following her mother's death. At the end of the weekend, it couldn't have been easy to return to the cramped duplex in Montreal that she shared with Fritz and baby Peter.

After meeting in 1929, Paul, Eleanor and Fritz socialized occasionally in Montreal. Paul even attended parties
at the Knechtel's apartment. But once Eleanor and Fritz
moved to the suburbs in 1934, Paul began to visit only
when Fritz was out of town. He'd arrive in the evenings
after Peter was asleep and could be left with a friend, and
would take Eleanor out in his car for a drive. They wrote
one another impassioned letters and met in Montreal
whenever she could get away.

Included in the divorce documents is an interview
with a man named Harry Napolean Sealander who
worked for my grandfather for two months as a "house-
man chauffeur." Sealander said that in the fall of 1934 he
prepared and served Eleanor and Paul an intimate dinner
at Mr. Smith's apartment. He wasn't officially introduced
to Eleanor at the time but heard Paul call her by name and
noticed the two were on "close terms," even acting "as man
and wife."

Attached to Sealander's interrogation in the file is a
black-and-white photograph of my grandparents. In it,
they are standing side by side on the steps of a white clap-
board house with a dog panting at their feet. There are
patches of snow on the ground. Paul has a pipe clenched
between his teeth and one hand resting on a shotgun.
Eleanor is looking off toward the edge of the photo, her
thick hair bobbed and curly. She is dressed for the bush
in big boots and men's pants cinched at the waist, a
figure-hugging sweater tucked in. Her lips are pursed
into a smile. They look at ease with one another but they
aren't touching. Sealander said he took the photo in
November 1934 when he drove them to a weekend get-
away at a country house near Shawinigan, Quebec. In the

divorce case both Eleanor and Paul claimed that it was during that weekend that "misconduct" first occurred between them.

A month after the photo was taken, however, Eleanor, Fritz and five-year-old Peter were gone. They abruptly left their house in Woodlands and moved back to Ontario. They had been summoned. For several months that summer and fall—the same time that Eleanor and Paul's romance heated up—the Knechtel company had veered close to collapse, thousands of employees' lives hanging in the balance. After the dismissal of a key union organizer in August, an informal strike had erupted.

It must have been a dreary Christmas at the Knechtel home, that winter of 1935. Fritz's father, J.S., had been forced to sell the vacation home in Florida. The club at Tamarac Island was the next to go. The strike, meanwhile, had drawn the workers and the community together. There was record-breaking attendance at the union's annual carnival at the local ice rink.

It would have been especially miserable for Eleanor. She knew she wanted to leave Fritz. She'd tried to do it before, when they were in Montreal, even packed her bags and headed for the door. Each time, he said that he would change, that they should try again. For Peter's sake. That Christmas he told her if she left, it would be permanent. She decided to wait until she had a plan.

Once the holidays were over, Fritz left for London, Ontario, where he planned to look for a house for the family. Eleanor and Peter went up to Wiarton to stay at her grandparents' home, then headed over to the cottage at Kee-am as soon as the weather was warm enough. Fritz came by when he could, but the marriage was strained. He and Eleanor hadn't even slept in the same bed for the better part of a year. She wrote love letters and poetry to Paul back in Montreal. One she dated May 22 borrows a few phrases and its metre from Edna St. Vincent Millay's well-known sonnet "Loving you less than life, a little less," but the sentiment is Eleanor's own.

> Knowing now that Life is plainer food
> Than first it seemed, when mist or song recall
> Far visions of a richer way, I would
> I need not swear I love you not at all.
> For there is that about this dull sane light
> That darkens and unwisely doubts the past,
> The while it tries to veil my straining sight
> From glimpse of you, and taunting, holds me fast.
> But I am made aware of many a week
> I shall consume, remembering in what way
> Your brown hair grows about your brow and cheek
> And what divine absurdities you say.
> Just shame will hold me lest I break a promise—
> But we dream most when dreams are farthest from us.

In May, Fritz intercepted a registered letter from Montreal with Eleanor's name on it, forging her signature at the local post office. In the letter Paul talked about running away to South America or South Africa. He called Eleanor "dearest in the world" and signed the letter "Always yours, my only love."

Whatever happened next is not recorded in the divorce record or family memory, but there must have been a confrontation. Fritz was livid about Eleanor's betrayal. She was furious he had invaded her privacy. They hurled cruelties at one another, made accusations. But still nothing happened right away. Fritz had to leave on business again. Eleanor and Peter stayed at the cottage, swimming at the beach and rowing in the little boat. Paul even stole away from Montreal, visiting secretly at Kee-am for a few days near the end of June.

By the beginning of August, Eleanor was desperate to make a move. She took six-year-old Peter to the Tyson house in Wiarton and said she'd be back in a few days to collect him. She reluctantly borrowed money from her brother Dick and headed down to Toronto to look for work to support herself and Peter. She didn't tell her husband anything.

When Fritz returned from his business trip and figured out that Eleanor had finally left him, he acted decisively. Eleanor was still in Toronto, so he went to Wiarton to the house on Tyson Street, gathered Peter's things and took the boy to stay at his brother's home in Hanover. He couldn't stop his wife from leaving him for another man but he wouldn't let her have the child, as well. The law would be on his side.

Since 1930, power to grant divorce, annulment, alimony and child custody in Ontario had been in the hands of the provincial Supreme Court. Before that, you had to have a private member's bill requesting it pass through the federal legislature. You had to have money, connections and proof of adultery. The new provincial process was easier to access and less expensive, but adultery was still the only grounds to end a marriage.

The complication for a woman seeking divorce was that if she admitted to an affair, she was considered little more than a whore. She would certainly be excluded from "polite" social circles. Only the year before Eleanor left Fritz, Group of Seven painter Lawren Harris and his second wife were driven out of Toronto in shame following his divorce. Even the United Church—which had pushed for the liberalizing of the legislation and which would later provide Eleanor a place within its fold—condemned remarriage between a divorcée and her lover.

But Eleanor must have felt she had no other option. In the divorce papers, she and Paul both readily acknowledge Fritz's allegations of infidelity. Paul even offers up the exact name, address and current employer of his former chauffeur, Harry Sealander, who could confirm their adultery— complete with a photo. It seems likely that the proceedings were at least partly scripted to speed the process. Indeed, there is the distinct sense that my grandfather's legal training is the invisible thread tying it all together. Proof of an affair was the only way that Eleanor could finally get away from the man she had grown to despise. In the eyes of the law, it also meant that she was an unfit mother.

Eleanor lived in Toronto while the divorce went through the courts. She rented a little apartment in a house on Spadina Road, up the hill near the enormous mock-castle known as Casa Loma. She found work at Eaton's department store in the copywriting department, writing blurbs promoting products. She probably had to lie about her marital status to get the job. It was still the depression and few companies were willing to hire a married woman, let alone an admitted adulteress.

Eleanor longed to get out of what she regarded as a tired, provincial city but she couldn't go anywhere until the divorce was final. She still harboured faint hope that Peter might come to live with her and Paul once they married.

Paul was talking about going straight to Montreal city hall after the divorce went through. It couldn't happen soon enough.

At the end of May 1936, less than a year after Eleanor walked out on Fritz, their marriage was over. Fritz got everything he asked for from Eleanor and Paul, including costs of the divorce action and full custody of the child.

In one of my grandmother's photo albums there is a page of photographs of her and six-year-old Peter. They were taken at Kee-am the summer before she left Fritz.

The scene in the pictures is idyllic. Peter is a golden boy, freckle-faced and missing his front teeth. He and his mother are laughing, wrapped in a hammock in front of the cabin, swimming in the bay at the front of the cottage. Peter looks happy, certain of himself. Kee-am—with the funny Murphy bed that looked like a china cabinet when upright and a moth-eaten bear rug on the floor—was a child's paradise. Eleanor recalled summer days there with her mother, sailing in pointy wooden skiffs, hamming it up for photographs with her cousins, arms slung lazily around each other's shoulders, pieces of straw sticking out of their laughing mouths. The cottage was the only place she remembered being happy when she was a child.

At night, as the sun sank into the line where water meets sky she snuggled Peter on the front porch and told him stories, dredging up things she thought she'd forgotten. Like the Crawford family favourite about the old bear rug. How once, on the trip from Tobermory up to Manitoulin, her father, Captain Jim, saw an enormous black bear swimming in the water. He wasn't much of a hunter, the story went, but the beast was so big and the shot so easy, that he got out a gun and took one shot, then another. The bear splashed and flailed. Dead. *Black as my hat*, Jim told everyone.

In the photographs of Peter and Eleanor, there's that elusive summer glow around them—the blur of long, warm days that always end too soon. Eleanor's hand cups Peter's cheek, pulling him affectionately toward her side; she digs her feet into the sand while the bare-bottomed boy stands in the foreground, looking over a brown shoulder at the camera and grinning. There's another of Peter in a one-piece striped wool swimsuit and white safari hat. He's standing military straight and holding a fishing pole like a Masai warrior, the lid to a giant cooking pot his shield.

It would be the last summer Eleanor and Peter would spend together at the cottage. The last time mother and son would be together ever again.

When the divorce was finalized, Fritz and Peter were living with the elder Knechtels at the old family home. Fritz continued to spend weeks at a time on the road; his parents and siblings watched out for the boy. Peter was discouraged from asking questions about his mother and wasn't allowed to contact her. Her letters to him were intercepted. At Christmas, Fritz relented and Peter was allowed to receive one gift. Each December after that the boy would watch the mail for a package from Montreal. One year she sent him a big globe of the world, the bumps of mountains and raised letters of countries like braille for the sighted. You could run your hand over the ridges, peaks and valleys. Everywhere he moved he brought it with him.

Eleanor and Paul didn't talk about her past to anyone. It became a family secret.

Chapter 15

THE GALL

IT WAS A BRIGHT, high-pressure August afternoon in 1972 the first time I visited Wiarton. The sun was playing hide-and-seek with a few cotton-batten clouds and a cool wind was blowing off Colpoy's Bay, whistling through the leaky walls of the old Victorian railway-station building and onto the grounds of Bluewater Park. I remember wanting to sprint away from the old people gathered there, away from the tension that had stolen all the air in our yellow station wagon on the trip over. I wanted to jump and splash on the beach but was told with an urgent hiss to keep quiet and be still.

I'd just had a birthday. My grandmother, aunt and cousins had arrived from Montreal the day before with presents. I didn't see them often and it was exciting. My grandmother Eleanor looked sophisticated and glamorous, as usual. She wore a tan-coloured swing coat. She'd left my grandfather Paul at home in Montreal, as she usually did when she came to visit us in Ontario.

But it wasn't my birthday they had all come to celebrate. The Salvation Army band in its freshly pressed uniforms and all the solemn-looking strangers gathered on the Wiarton lakefront weren't there for me.

After a brassy rendition of "O Canada" the mayor cleared her throat and welcomed everyone to the unveiling of a plaque commemorating the terrible wreck of Wiarton's own S.S. *J. H. Jones*. She was especially pleased, she said, nodding in our direction, to welcome the surviving family of Captain James Victor Crawford, and the relatives of other passengers and crew who were lost on the *Jones*. My grandmother, who sat two chairs away from me, was looking down at the ground, flattening the grass with her shoe. Her brothers Dick and Whit stared straight ahead, pursing their lips and shaking their heads slightly in the way people do to acknowledge something important but unspeakable. Peggy wasn't able to make it from her home in the Nevada desert but Bert, the eldest Crawford at eighty-one years old, was sitting up front with the dignitaries. All three brothers seemed ancient to me. It was hard to imagine these small, shrunken men connected to my stylish grandmother.

The local MP followed the mayor, speaking about "The last days of the *J. H. Jones*." Then two other men talked about what they called Wiarton's Great Disaster. Finally, it was Bert's turn. With a small flourish he lifted the black draping, unveiling a sturdy metal plaque with raised letters: "This seaworthy. . .wooden freight and passenger ship built at Goderich. . .was owned by Crawford Tug Co. Wiarton, and captained by James V. Crawford and a crew of. . .Wiarton men. . . ."

Someone read the names of the passengers and crew out loud like a roll call as we all sat silently in chairs the local funeral home had lent for the occasion. Then, just as I thought I couldn't sit still another second, the band struck up a hymn, and the Reverend Thomas A. Scott of Wiarton's Anglican church directed us all to stand. "Eternal Father strong to save," boomed the crowd, their voices caught in the wind and hurtled up a gentle rise toward the main street of town. "Oh, hear us when we cry to Thee,/ For those in peril on the sea!"

When the hymn was over, the hundred or so people scattered. Dick, Whit, Bert and their families walked slowly over to the railway building, picking their steps carefully in the patchy grass. We followed behind, my grandmother clutching her two daughters' hands. My cousin and I grabbed hands, too, swinging them wildly between us.

It had never occurred to me that my grandmother had family other than us, let alone a father who died at sea. It was hard to believe that she had ever been a little girl like me, running around barefoot, being chased by her brothers, swung into the air by her father, swimming and splashing in Georgian Bay. As far as I could see she'd barely spoken to her siblings yet and we'd been at the park for several hours. I learned later that it was the first time she'd seen any of them in decades.

* * *

Eleanor's family in Wiarton was appalled and embarrassed by her divorce and the affair that caused it. Aunt Susie was mortified that she had played a role, looking after Peter while Eleanor ran off to the city. Dick was angry that he'd lent her all that money when she had a big-city lawyer for a boyfriend. But it wasn't really that surprising, many in the family said; Eleanor had always been ambitious. She'd just traded up when Fritz turned out not to be the high flyer she thought she'd married.

It wasn't the sort of behaviour that was easily forgiven in Wiarton. One was expected to accept one's place. Loyalty and humility were prized above all. People moved away, of course, they might even marry well, but they knew better than to flaunt it with fancy clothes and interesting, exotic lives.

Even today there are relatives who remember my grandmother with a whiff of disapproval. She hitched her wagon to a star, one of her cousins told me. She liked nice clothes—though her mother couldn't afford them, some-one added. Others remembered her as a snob. She was a social climber, her brother Dick told his friends.

After the divorce Eleanor had little to do with her family, save letters to her sister Peggy and a few favourite cousins her own age. My mother and aunt visited Wiarton only twice when they were children. I had no idea that we still had relatives in the area until I began to look for them myself. When I did track them down, these cousins and in-laws were all kind to me, helpful and interested in my search, but I still felt as if talking about my grandmother was treading on sensitive territory.

In some of these discussions, I found myself trying to set the record straight about why she ran away from her small town as soon as she could, why she married Fritz and then left him. I reminded them about the blame cast over her father and how everything changed for the Crawford family after the wreck of the *Jones*; about how she felt that long before her divorce and fall from grace, she was treated with suspicion by people in Wiarton. If I detected even a hint of censure, I had to restrain myself from rushing to her defence. I feel protective of her, responsible somehow. It is part of my inheritance—my pirate on the family tree.

And yet I can't help thinking that my grandmother would find my reaction silly. She didn't see herself as needing a defender when she was alive and she certainly doesn't need one now. She made difficult decisions about her life and rarely looked back. She shaped herself—and her legacy—exactly how she saw fit.

When I was nine years old, she gave me something that I was told was very special. It came wrapped in crispy brown paper, the stiff waxy kind with lines running through it. It was a lace handkerchief that had been starched flat, placed on a mat of royal-blue velvet and framed. The lace was exquisite, knots and loops forming a delicate, spiky border around a linen square in the middle. A plaque of thick watercolour paper covered in my grandmother's neat calligraphy had been attached to the front, on top of the glass. On it was written in perfect, evenly spaced script: "Handmade Battenberg Lace made by Jane Kelly, sister of Elizabeth Kelly Tyson, mother of Lilias Tyson Crawford*, mother of Eleanor Crawford Smith*, mother of Erica Smith Curtis*, mother of Andrea Curtis. *Carried at their weddings."

The lace hung on my wall until my parents sold the house I grew up in a few years ago. I must have read the description thousands of times. When I was young, I was impressed by the age of the lace, and the fact that the woman who made it was related to me. Later I would wonder more at the certainty of the words, at how easy it is to edit a life, to avoid mention of the tangled marriages and tragedies of the women who carried the small square of fabric.

Several years ago, my mother, who'd given up on me getting married, told me that more than anything else she was sorry to see that piece of lace remain forever behind glass. I had never imagined myself as a bride, let alone one carrying a lace hanky, and I laughed. But she didn't think it was funny. It was important to her, more important than I knew at the time: a link to her mother, to her mother's lost family, and to me. So when my boyfriend and I surprised everyone with the news that we were going to get married—on a rock, in the middle of Georgian Bay—the handkerchief was hauled out and carefully removed from its frame.

On the day of the ceremony in the last-minute frenzy, I almost forgot the lace. I can still hear one of my friends screaming faux-dramatically, "The hanky! The hanky!" as I headed out the door. But it was found just in time and I happily carried it in my hand. I was glad to have something of my grandmother with me. My mother was teary-eyed at the ceremony, beaming from her perch near the front of the small crowd.

My grandparents were married in May 1936 at the Erskine and American United Church in Montreal. It was less than a week after Eleanor and Fritz's marriage was officially dissolved. She and Paul had decided that there was no time to waste. The Canadian Senate was considering a bill that would make it illegal for the "guilty" party in a divorce to marry during the lifetime of his or her "innocent" spouse. It was now or never.

Eleanor dressed carefully in a smart white suit with gathered sleeves and matching hat. Paul topped his natty pinstriped, double-breasted suit with a white fedora. It was a small ceremony, with a reception afterward in the garden of Paul's Hutchison Avenue apartment. There was no one there to represent Eleanor's side of the family. Paul's siblings and their spouses came, but his parents were less enthusiastic.

May and Walter Smith were not pleased about their eldest son's choice. May, especially, thought the girl was a bad influence. He had such promise—to have had an affair and then to marry a divorcée seemed like a squandering of opportunity. Doors would surely be closed to him. There would be people who wouldn't want to hire such a lawyer. If they had children, they would undoubtedly be deformed. And if by some good fortune they had normal babies, there would be parents who wouldn't want their darlings playing with the offspring of such a union.

More importantly, divorce was sacrilege. May Smith was a believer in religious visions. She told her children that since the age of seven she had witnessed at least eight miracles. When she realized Paul was serious about marrying Eleanor she prayed constantly for a sign from God to tell her what to do.

At the last minute, she and Walter decided to attend their eldest son's wedding. May still had reservations but she put them aside for the moment. In a letter she wrote to Eleanor she explained, "We all love Paul, and I am sure he would not be happy if we were not friends, so that I will not talk of an attitude, beliefs or prejudices, but start from here."

Still, it would take time before Eleanor was completely accepted by the family. She was unfazed. She was happy, for once, and convinced she could win over the Smiths.

And, indeed, Paul's brothers and sisters found Eleanor charming and gracious. She was such a tremendously chic and dashing figure that one of her sisters-in-law remembers when she visited Montreal from her small town, she would always carry high heels in a little bag, *just in case* she ran into Eleanor. Another sister-in-law recalls the day they were out shopping together when a man pulled his car to a screeching halt to exclaim: "What an amazing hat!"

Over the years, May Smith also came to love Eleanor. May was an accomplished artist as well as a gardener, and the two women encouraged one another. For her part, May was grateful that Eleanor could keep Paul in line—which was more than anyone in his family could say. One word from Eleanor and he would stop arguing in midsentence. When he drank too much, she'd make sure he didn't offend anyone. On his own, they all agreed, Paul might have drifted away from his family. Eleanor made certain that they visited Duldreaggan Hall often and stayed in touch with his siblings. The Smiths became her family, too.

Paul and Eleanor didn't talk about her past to anyone. Their affair and her divorce were never mentioned.

She had virtually no contact with Peter other than her cards and gifts to him at Christmas and birthdays. When my aunt Paula was born, four years after their wedding, there was no looking back. Eleanor's other life became a family secret.

When nine-year-old Peter became seriously ill, it must have strained Paul and Eleanor's tacit agreement about leaving the past in the past. Rosalina Knechtel contacted Eleanor after the boy's temperature had soared in the stratosphere for a full week. He was delirious. Doctors couldn't figure out what was wrong with him. His father's sister Xenia, a nurse trained at Johns Hopkins in Baltimore, stayed constantly by his bedside. Everyone thought he would die.

Finally, the Hanover doctors diagnosed him with an acute infection, which had found its way from a blister on his foot into his femur and was slowly depriving the bone of its blood supply. He was sent immediately to the Hospital for Sick Children in Toronto to endure the first of three operations that would leave him bedridden for much of the next three years and with difficulty walking for the rest of his life. When he emerged from the haze of ether following the operation, he asked Fritz if his mother could visit. The answer was no.

For both Peter and Eleanor there would have been no questioning such an edict. She had no rights in his regard— Fritz was Peter's sole guardian. But it must have been confusing and lonely for the boy, extraordinarily painful for his mother. She wouldn't have missed the tragic irony. Absence and loss had also been the defining quality of her childhood. The sense of abandonment she had worked so furiously to escape had come back to haunt not just her, but her son.

* * *

Whenever I think about my grandmother's life, it is the fact that she never again saw her child after the divorce that I have most difficulty understanding. Now that I have a son of my own, the notion is even more incomprehensible to me. Knowing her circumstances, her history, the social climate of the time, I still can't get my head around the fact that she had no choice in the matter. I can't help feeling she should have tried harder. Perhaps one of those consequences of remembering one's history is not being able to forgive it.

I've asked my mother often about how Eleanor made sense of the situation. But she had never dared probe that hard. She was told about the existence of a half-brother in a matter-of-fact sort of way when she was fifteen. She knew that the boy had been raised by an aunt and was, by the time she learned about him, a grown man. The fact of him didn't touch my mother's teenage self much—there was certainly no talk of meeting him—but it did force her to recall a childhood memory: when she was little, she used to sneak into her parents' room to look in a little-used dresser drawer. There she'd puzzle over a studio portrait of her mother holding a cherubic-looking blond boy. Her mother was young and pretty in the photo, smiling indulgently at the mysterious child.

Not long after my grandmother died, my mother and aunt decided to contact Peter. They tracked him down through a cousin. It was the first time they'd ever spoken. He said that he'd heard about their mother's death from another relative. He was retired, he explained, never married, still living in Hanover. He spoke of his childhood illnesses and explained how Aunt Xenia, his own maiden aunt, had become like a mother to him. Eleanor was little more than a long-ago memory, a faded picture, a once-a-year present. He said he was sorry for their loss.

My mother has kept in touch with Peter over the years, writing Christmas cards and even meeting with him a few times. Several years ago, she went with me when I visited him at the assisted care facility where he now lives. He's had various illnesses over the years and needs help occasionally. He uses a wheelchair to get around. About a month before we visited, he'd had a minor stroke and his speech was slightly slurred, though he was sharp, as usual, his bright blue eyes flashing in delight at some detail he recalled.

We sat out in the garden courtyard while he ate his lunch and told stories. Peter has the mannerisms of a man who hasn't had to accommodate himself much to other people's needs. He has a verbal quirk that sounds like *hmmmm?*, which he employs every few sentences. It is posed as a question but it's really a rhetorical pause. He doesn't like interruptions. I'd heard most of what he told us before, and had some specific questions this time, but he ran through his life story from top to bottom, anyway.

He told us how he lived with his father, aunt, uncle and cousins in his grandparents' house when he was boy. He said that his father never remarried and worked as a salesman for the family company until he lost a leg as a result of poor circulation. Peter told us that after spending so much of his childhood in hospital, he'd wanted to be a doctor when he grew up, but discovered in university that it was too much work. He explained that his father and the rest of the Knechtel family didn't try to intentionally poison him against his mother, but they wouldn't let him see her, either. He was not to ask questions about her. He added irritably that if I was hoping to hear he'd pined away his life, resenting his father, wishing his mother would come back for him, I'd come to the wrong place.

It felt strange to talk to him about Eleanor. He'd barely known the person who gave birth to him and raised him for six years—the same woman who had so affected my life and my mother's. He evidently feels a connection to her, but it is unnameable, even maddening. For my mother and for me, the conversation was also tinged with an odd sort of guilt, for we are the beneficiaries of her abandonment of him.

But mostly it felt strange because Peter carries his mother in his face. Their resemblance is uncanny. He has the large, square-shaped head that is a Crawford trademark, the same wide forehead I have seen in studio portraits of Captain Jim. He has my grandmother's nose and her lovely soft cheeks and skin. I can see her sense of mischief—the girl who startled Wiarton with a jump in the ice-bound bay when she was a teenager, the grown woman who stopped traffic with her dramatic hats—in his restless, intelligent eyes.

Looking at him sitting in the garden, he was at once deeply familiar to me and entirely alien—as contradictory and elusive as any of the other artifacts of my grandmother's life.

Eleanor didn't write much after she married my grandfather Paul. Perhaps she didn't have the time or mental space once my aunt and mother were born. Or maybe she found it too risky. Her poetry had been the written manifestation of her desire to break free of the confines of her life, of her dissatisfaction with what was expected of her. After the trauma of the divorce, and her remarriage, she was determined to create a life with Paul, to have normalcy. She had too much to lose to take chances with the emotion that might emerge if she put pen to paper. She'd discovered the hard way that for a woman of her generation, the price of nonconformity was very high.

She found other outlets for her creative energy. She designed costumes for the Montreal Ballet, she sewed clothing for her children. She arranged flowers for the Château du Ramezay and the McCord Museum; she did needlepoint. She liked to keep her hands busy. There was a time when for all occasions her grandchildren would receive stones painted as ladybugs or decorative eggs. Another time she got very into découpage and each person in the family was given personalized boxes and vases covered in milky layers of glue and magazine clippings.

Just as she had set herself to winning over the Smiths, Eleanor put her mind to establishing a stable, middle-class life for herself and her family. She enrolled her daughters in figure skating and ballet lessons, instilled in them a careful sense of what was right and proper, encouraged them to explore intellectual interests but expected that they would marry well. She volunteered, even becoming the president of the Montreal Volunteer Bureau and the Women's Auxiliary of the Montreal General Hospital. She joined the United Church, and became an active member of the Mount

Royal congregation. She designed and sewed banners for special church occasions, was involved in committees and clubs, including a small group that met regularly for "intellectual discussions" and community service.

She looked after her husband and daughters, their modest home in the Town of Mount Royal, the secluded cabin they built in the woods on the Quebec side of the Ottawa River not far from Hawkesbury. She was loyal and strong-minded, admired for her diplomacy and ability to relate to people from different backgrounds. And she was always perfectly turned out.

This, of course, was the grandmother I knew and admired. Hers had been a good life, even an admirable one, but it wasn't the romantic tale she had carefully fostered as a young woman. She wasn't the mysterious and fascinating Eleanor who emerged from my mother's stories and the package of poems, letters and photographs my aunt sent me—the one whose life I had been given to tell. It was the rebellious and artistic girl who became the heroine of her own life that I had built my imagination on. I think I hoped that one day I might be like that, too.

There's a ring of hers that I've kept in my desk drawer for years that always reminds me of this. I try it on sometimes, holding my hand out at arm's length, imagining it on her slender, crooked fingers. The rock is gold, the shape of an egg and it rests in an ordinary silver setting of twisting leaves. It's big for a ring, but not unlike a lot of the costume jewellery she favoured. If you didn't know, you'd never imagine that it is a gallstone my grandmother painted gold and mounted.

When she was in her sixties she had a gallbladder operation that produced several of these large stones. The attacks had been extraordinarily painful and she was relieved to finally get them out, so when the doctor asked if she'd like to see the source of her agony, she figured she'd get a good hard look. I'm not certain what compelled her to then glue one in a ring, but I've always thought it was hilarious, a glorious flaunting of convention, shocking and strangely witty at the same time, a not-so-gentle poke at our collective discomfort with illness. I love the idea of a sixty-something Montreal matron doing something so outrageous. I think of the ring as The Gall. Aunt Susie would have been properly shocked.

My mother is vaguely embarrassed by it, but I cling to the ridiculous ring rather sentimentally. I think of it as a symbol of my grandmother's resistance, evidence of her stubborn defiance, of her courage to release herself from the rigid expectations of her time. It's a slight object to carry so much freight, but it's important to me that she had this free-spirited, non-conformist side. I hold on to it because it pains me to think that she felt she had no choice but to conform. And I can't allow the possibility that her message to me is that even the most courageous women have to acquiesce to social pressure. The ring tells me what I want to hear. Despite her adherence to things she was so adamantly against as a young woman—traditional female roles, the Church—she never really gave up the fight. I suppose I need to see her that way.

In my last year of university, my mother asked my aunt to paint a portrait of me. Aunt Paula had done one of her own daughter, one of my mother as a young woman and another of my grandmother. I would be part of the third generation of women in the family to sit for her.

I protested a bit. It was my last semester at McGill and I couldn't imagine being still, unable to read, study, write or even watch TV for the ten hours my aunt said it would take. I grumbled to my mother that I had too much work, that we should wait until I *at least* had a B.A. to immortalize me with a portrait. I successfully put off the sitting until a few months before I graduated when we all realized it would be the last opportunity before I left Montreal.

My aunt chose the background: a red woven cloth that she draped from an open closet door, a stack of books to rest on and represent my emerging interest in writing. I wore a plunging white shirt, a colourful Indian vest that incorporated tiny mirrors into the stitching and a big jade ring that had been my aunt's when she was my age. She would set me up on a platform in the hallway of her Montreal home, natural light flooding the space, then arrange my hands and knees, tilt my head and begin.

I look old in the nearly life-size painting, older perhaps than I am even now. My eyes are serious and dark, my fingers droop languidly over the books. It's not that it isn't a good likeness—the portrait is deeply textured, the colours restrained but rich—it's that there is also a hint of my mother who everyone says I look so much like, a glimmer of the grandmother whose passions I share.

I can easily transport myself back to the hours and weeks I sat for the painting. The oddly crumbling lethargy that entered my bones with my aunt's first gaze, the intensity of her stare the only thing holding my back straight. I remember the disconcerting feeling of being intimately observed, as if she was seeing me more clearly than anyone had ever seen me before. I felt overcome by emotions I couldn't name. It took all my will to keep at bay the tears that gathered like a line squall in the corners of my eyes. But the thing I recall most decisively is the feeling that I was being painted into existence, a new addition to the family story.

*There's a lightness out on the water, a sense of possibility
untethered by earthbound expectations.*

Chapter 16

"THE DEEP WATERS OF GEORGIAN BAY NEVER GIVE UP THEIR DEAD"

WHEN MY AUNT sent me the package of my grandmother's poems and letters, it seemed clear to me that I was to *do something* with it. In the stories my mother had spun, my grandmother was a person whose life was self-evidently worthy of note. It seemed obvious that I should write about her.

I quickly discovered that there is nothing obvious about family stories. There is much passed down, but important things are left out, other bits polished and refined in the telling, dramas created, stories edited for glamour or glory or shame. Whenever I think I know something for certain, I discover a new detail that alters the picture entirely. Things go in and out of focus, are illuminated, then disappear into the darkness before I can clutch them, make them my own.

Hoping to strip away these conflicting demands, the muddled self-interest, the pride and censure—and knowing, finally, that it was the closest I would get to that pirate on my family tree—I decided that I would go out on the water of Georgian Bay and track the final journey of the *J. H. Jones* for myself.

The fall light was golden when I set out from Owen Sound with my husband, my father and a family friend, the trees flickering red and orange, the shoreline fuzzy in movement like the edges of a dream. From the stern of our little fishing boat, we could see the grain elevator and oil storage tanks that mark opposite sides of the harbour entrance, the red-brick town just beyond. The *Chi-Cheemaun* car ferry, which winters at the mouth of the Sydenham River, was docked there, laid up for the season. In summer, the 365-foot ship travels The Gap between Tobermory at the tip of the Bruce and South Baymouth on Manitoulin Island, carrying tourists and their vehicles. It is the last holdout of nearly two centuries of passenger boats on this side of Georgian Bay.

The wind on the water in the sound was fresh, stirring up brisk whitecaps that rose and fell with artillery precision. It was still warm. The Arctic winds of fall had yet to blow into Georgian Bay.

Our boat was outfitted with GPS and a depth sounder; we also had the latest charts installed on a laptop plugged into the cigarette lighter on the dashboard. But we didn't really need any of it. The trip out Owen Sound, past Colpoy's Bay and on to Cape Croker is straightforward. We would stay offshore a bit to avoid any shallow parts, but the water is generally quite deep and clear.

The sound is twelve miles long but motoring along in our small boat it seemed longer. I'd been staring at a map of this passage for months by then, measuring the progress of the *Jones* in inches and shades of pink and blue. It was exhilarating to be out on the water, to see with my own eyes what my great-grandfather had seen, to feel the wind and roll of the waves.

I was also just a bit uneasy about the morbid journey we were on, even slightly superstitious, as though our pilgrimage might stir the wrath of the bay that still hasn't "given up" the *Jones*.

We hugged the northwest shore of the sound as we headed toward the open. There was a spectacular view of the southeast coast: the army firing range and tank exercise area on the hill just west of Cape Rich; the eerie mound of Coffin Hill; the Claybanks, with its dun-coloured cliffs, just beyond.

Halfway to the mouth of the sound we passed Presqu'ile, where a lighthouse once guided mariners into a tiny village. I remembered as we motored by that the *Asia* stopped there on its tragic final journey, stocking up on cordwood to feed her hungry boilers. Today, the village's store and telegraph company, the temperance hotel, post office, blacksmith shop, cooperage and tin smithy are all gone. Near the old lighthouse there are the modern-looking buildings of a youth camp.

As the bay widened and we emerged from the shelter of the shore, the wind began to pick up. It was there at

Cape Commodore that Jim Crawford and his crew would have had their first inkling of the storm's strength.

We were faced with only a warm west wind. The lull of the waves was hypnotic, reminding me of long summer days with my parents on our sailboat, *Peacetrain*. I loved heading to the open water, watching the shore drop out of sight, seeing the water stretch blue and grey into the horizon. If it wasn't too windy, I'd perch myself on the metal bowsprit that poked out in front of the boat, hooking my legs around the rail, feet dangling over the water. Sitting there with the sound of crashing water, the wind pushing my hair off my forehead, nothing to see but water and the occasional arc of a seagull's wing, I imagined I was alone in the world.

The water that is my consolation was my grandmother's nightmare. I have often thought about the irony in the fact that after all Eleanor did to leave this place—this water—her daughter not only returned to it, she fell in love with a man, my father, whose passion is sailing, a man whose own family story is intimately tied to Georgian Bay. It's probably mostly coincidence, partly the pull of demography and economics, but, I wondered as we charged through the growing waves, if it's also the force of the past moving in the present, dragging and tugging, aching like a phantom limb.

It's the sort of thinking that can come easily out on the water, free of the peculiar weight of land: the buildings and pavement, the urgent press of human need. It must have been something like this feeling that my great-grandfather and other sailors longed for in the early spring after the boredom and closeness of winter on shore. A lightness and sense of possibility, of being untethered by earthbound expectations.

Up ahead, I spotted the lighthouse at Griffith Island. It's one of six so-called Imperial Towers on the Bruce, constructed in the 1850s out of enormous limestone blocks quarried near Owen Sound. There's a small abandoned-looking stone house nearby.

When the *Jones* passed by there in November 1906, William Boyd was the keeper. In newspaper accounts of the wreck, Boyd noted that when the *Jones* steamed by the tower she was making good time. He said that because it was cloudy and blowing, he couldn't actually see the boat very well.

For us, too, the wind began to pick up more once we passed the Griffith Island lighthouse. We were no longer protected by the peninsula, and the waves were growing. They were steeper and closer together than before. Our little boat was getting pitched around. As we crashed down off a wave, cold spray hit us like shrapnel.

There had been another sighting of the *Jones* nearby. Some local fishermen saw her making her way north of the island. In the tense days after the wreck, they told newspaper reporters and everyone else that though she was buffeted by the waves, when the *Jones* passed them she was riding the storm as well as she usually did. They watched as Captain Jim and his men steered the steamer through the narrow troughs of the increasingly heavy seas, white spray dashing over the hurricane deck and breaking around the pilothouse.

Not far in the distance, I could see the wooded thickness of Hay Island and then Cape Croker. The cape is a finger that pokes vehemently out into the bay. From our boat it looked dark and cold, like a sheer rock fortress. I've been to the lighthouse that sits at its bitter end, the place where the *Jones* was last seen. It's a lonely spot, a grey rocky beach below the tower and nothing but water into the sky. There wasn't even a road out there in 1906. The keeper, Richard Chapman, and his family would arrive by boat in April and leave the same way in December.

Our trip was taking much longer than I had imagined. We'd been going for several hours by then and we were only a bit more than halfway to our destination around the north side of Cape Croker. The waves were slowing us down. We were wet and beginning to get tired from bracing our bodies against the smash as our boat slammed down off the peak of a wave. I began to realize that it wouldn't take a lot for something to go wrong and flip us over or swamp the boat. There was no one else out there and the water was cold. I imagined the newspaper headlines describing the hubris of our demise in pursuit of a long-lost shipwreck.

The howling wind began to sound like voices to me. It didn't help that the previous few nights I'd had dreams about my grandmother. I'd wake up and struggle in the half-light of morning to make sense of them, to untangle what was real and what was imagined, what was about her and what was really about me. During the day I'd found myself making guesses about something or other that she or someone else had done, and then, in my research, find that I was actually, uncannily correct. It was exciting to be so absorbed in something that everything felt connected, to discover that my intuition was right. But out on the bay, with the wind whipping the water into tangled sheets of barbed wire, the dreams and connections began to feel more like a warning.

I struggled momentarily with the siren call of the open bay, then suggested we head for shelter. I didn't think we needed to risk our lives for this task. I have tried to map my grandmother's life, negotiating the shoals of falseness and fabrication. I have tried to make sense of what her father and the *Jones* meant in her life, of her legacy to me. But I have never thought I was a captive of this history.

Heading south, away from Cape Croker and the water that swallowed the *J. H. Jones,* the wind was behind us, the waves mellow. We turned in behind the islands and came out at the village of Big Bay on the shore near Oxenden. Jumping out onto the dock, it felt like I was still in motion, bouncing on the waves, as if my body hadn't yet caught up with gravity. I was relieved to be there. We ate our picnic lunch and dried off in the warm sun. We could see the waves out on the open water, the flash of whitecaps like thousands of jagged teeth bared in a grimace.

In our little bay, the water was calm; a rocky beach with pebbles the size of a sparrow stretched out beside the dock. I picked up a stone and skipped it. One, two, three times it skimmed across the water, bouncing into the air, the white rock catching the light of the sun, then dropping silently, heavily into the dark water.

IMAGE CREDITS

Except where noted, the photographs are courtesy of the Curtis and Gillett families. Every effort has been made to contact copyright holders. In the event of an error or omission, please notify the publisher.

The woodcut that appears at the opening of each chapter is from the letterhead and stock certificates of the Crawford Tug Company Ltd. Image courtesy of Thomas Crawford.

p. 2   The *J. H. Jones*, from a postcard.
p. 18   Captain James Victor Crawford. Photo courtesy of Thomas Crawford.
p. 32   Albert Munroe Tyson.
p. 48   Lillie Elizabeth Tyson and James Victor Crawford, probably taken for their engagement.
p. 58   Wiarton harbour, from a postcard. Reproduced courtesy of the Toronto Public Library (PC-2145).
p. 74   The *Crawford*. From a postcard made from a photograph in the collection of the late R. M. Crawford.

p. 92   Owen Sound harbour c. 1890. Photograph
        courtesy of Grey County Archives.

p. 112 The captain and crew of the *J. H. Jones* c. 1905.
        Identified as back row, left to right: James
        Tilley, Ed Lennox, Frank Jackson, Fred
        Wright, Doug Ewing and George Smith.
        Front row: Charles Shaw, Tom Simmons,
        Captain James V. Crawford, Wesley Sadler
        and William Ross. Fred Wright and Doug
        Ewing were the only two not on the *Jones*
        when she disappeared. Image reproduced from
        Wiarton's Great Disaster, 1972, Bruce County
        Historical Society.

p. 130 John Macaulay. Photo courtesy of Sue Scott.

p. 150 Lillie Crawford, centre, with Dick, left, and
        Madge.

p. 166 Jonathan Dowler, with his children Patricia
        (left) and Garvey at Pointe au Baril. Photo
        courtesy of Dorinda Keith.

p. 256 Shawanaga Inlet, Georgian Bay. Photo courtesy
        of Dorinda Keith.

Acknowledgements

This book would never have been written were it not for the insight, imagination and co-operation of my mother, Erica Curtis, and my aunt, Paula Gillett. It is my hope that I have been faithful to the stories they shared with me and to the generous spirit of their mother, Eleanor. I am deeply indebted to both of them for their love and encouragement, and for helping me understand that everyone has their own story to tell.

My father, James Curtis, was an eagle-eyed reader and tireless researcher, hunting down obscure details with his trademark tenacity. His enthusiasm for (nearly) everything I do amazes and inspires me.

Thanks must also be extended to the family members I discovered in researching my grandmother's life: Thomas Crawford, who was an ally and font of genealogical information from the very beginning; Susan and Don McCallum in Wiarton for their kindness and hospitality; Peter Knechtel, who was patient with my questions; also Dianne Breton, Bill Clarkson, Eleanor Crawford, John Curtis, Angie Dawson, Alwynn Gillett, Christopher Gillett, Phyllis Eleanor Hoehne, Frances Richardson,

Margaret Smith, Cynthia Taylor, Jack and Jeannette Tyson, and Robin Ward.

Others also helped out generously along the way. Sue Scott opened up her home and family albums; Ron Beaupre was unstinting with his time and remarkable archive of marine photographs; Peter McCutcheon took me on an eerie spring tour of the beaches of Christian Island; Roger Green shared his knowledge of Georgian Bay and made the fall weather seem less daunting; Geoff Mann dug in the Berkeley rare books library when I couldn't; Geoff Coulson took the time to walk me through the mind-boggling weather maps of 1906. Patrick Folkes, George Heigenhauser, Gordon Lawson, and the ever-patient and helpful librarians and archivists at the Toronto Reference Library, the Archives of Ontario, the Grey County Archives and the Bruce County museum at Southampton helped fill in many of the gaps. Thank you all.

There are a few books and journals that I returned to again and again that bear noting. On Georgian Bay and Bruce Peninsula history—James Barry's *Georgian Bay: The Sixth Great Lake*, Ruth McCuaig's *Our Pointe au Baril*, W. Sherwood Fox's *The Bruce Beckons*, the Great Lakes journal *Inland Seas* and the unpublished boyhood reminiscences of the late Frederick Gourlay Millar each provided important pieces of the puzzle. The two booklets on the wreck of the *Jones* were essential reading: *Wiarton's Great Disaster* and Patrick Folkes's *The Saddest Calamity*. On weather and navigation, *Eric Sloan's Weather Book*, Environment Canada's *Wind, Weather & Waves*, *Sea Sense* by Richard Henderson and *Boating in Canada* by Garth

Griffiths were invaluable. Joy Parr's *The Gender of Breadwinners* and W. H. Graham's remarkable *Greenbank: Country Matters in 19th Century Ontario* helped make historical sense of my family story.

I am grateful also to my first readers: Bronwen Low, Sophie McCall, Rosemary Renton and Joanne Saul, who understood what I wanted to do from the beginning and talked me through many lapses in courage and judgment. They can't imagine how much I've depended on their creativity and wise counsel. Thanks also to Steve Brearton, Kathy Ceroni, Stephanie Garrow, Heather Gellatly, Stephen Gregory, Liz Kingston, Katie Macaulay and Lisa Werlich for their many kindnesses. I am also extraordinarily grateful to Pat and John Saul whose generosity know no bounds.

Thank you to my agent, Jackie Kaiser, who ably steered me through the labyrinthine world of book publishing and was enthusiastic from the start. And to the good people at Random House Canada, especially Kendall Anderson, Craig Pyette and my friend and editor Anne Collins, whose smart questions and vision for the book led me places I never imagined going.

I would also like to thank the Ontario Arts Council Writer's Reserve program, the Toronto Arts Council and the Canada Council for their support.

Finally, my greatest debt is to Ben, whose interrogations about ghosts and shipwrecks made me ask myself what I really know, and whose capacity for empathy astounds me daily; and to Nicholas, whose patience, love and innate optimism make anything seem possible. All love.

ANDREA CURTIS is a National Magazine Award winner and has worked as an editor and writer at *This Magazine, Toronto Life* and *Shift*. She lives in Toronto. *Into the Blue* is her first book.